The Stranger

THE STRANGER

THE MACMILLAN COMPANY
NEW YORK · BOSTON · CHICAGO · DALLAS
ATLANTA · SAN FRANCISCO

MACMILLAN & CO., LIMITED
LONDON · BOMBAY · CALCUTTA ·
MELBOURNE

THE MACMILLAN CO. OF CANADA, LTD.
TORONTO

THE STRANGER

BY
ARTHUR BULLARD

Author of
"A Man's World," "Comrade Yetta," "The
Barbary Coast," "The Russian
Pendulum," etc.

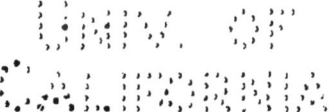

New York
THE MACMILLAN COMPANY
1920

TABLE OF CONTENTS

427941

From a dialogue between Alcuin of York, Philosopher-in-ordinary to Charlemagne, and Pepin, the Emperor's son.

Pepin: "What is Life?"

Alcuin: "The joy of the Happy—
The Expectation of Death."

Pepin: "What is Death?"

Alcuin: "An inevitable Event—an uncertain Journey—
Tears for the Living—the Thief of Man."

Pepin: "What is Man?"

Alcuin: "The Slave of Death—
A passing Traveler—
A Stranger in his own abode."

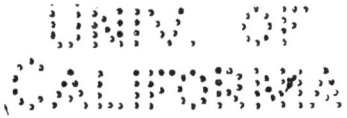

THE STRANGER

CHAPTER I

THE STRANGER IS ANNOUNCED

"Wasn't Eunice well enough to come to-night?"

There was a note of affectionate concern in Frank Lockwood's voice as he asked about the missing guest.

"Yes," Lillian, his wife, echoed, somewhat more perfunctorily. "How is Eunice?"

Although the table had been set for six, there were but two guests, Helen Cash and Winslow Mathews. Helen, who shared an apartment with Eunice Bender, answered, and her voice, which was ordinarily resonant and assured, sounded dreary.

"Nothing serious. No better, no worse. She had a wrangle with the printer this afternoon and was too tired to come out again."

Eunice was so dear to them all that a constraint and silence fell on them for a moment. Lillian was the first to break it.

"Pete," she said, "telegraphed at the last minute that he had to stay in Albany."

This started the conversation on the prospects of getting some reform bills through the legislature in this 1913 session. It was this work which had kept Peter McGee from joining them. It interested Helen very intimately in her own work. "Win" Mathews, who was McGee's close friend and roommate, was also deeply interested. Frank, who was an artist, less so, and Lillian not at all.

It was a tiny dining room, quite full with the four of them — it would have been crowded with six. When the house had been built a couple of generations ago, this room had been planned as a "back parlor." In those prosperous days, when the district had been fashionable, the large room behind had been the dining room, but when Frank and Win had come to the city together, ten years earlier, they had found the house crowded with a dozen Italian families. These had been dispossessed, and Frank had turned the original dining room into a studio.

This little room where they sat had only one window, looking out on a narrow air shaft, but it was amply supplied with doors — double, sliding doors, fore and aft, leading into the parlor and studio, and a single door, opposite the obscured window, into the hallway. Its very smallness rendered it cozy and intimate, and it was made gay by some oils on the wall — sketches by some of Frank's friends. There was none of his work there.

The table, set very formally, in an uptown, conventional way — a manner obviously inspired by the popular fashion magazines — seemed out of tune with the Bohemian setting. So did the hostess. Lillian was beautiful. She was beautifully gowned, for the advice of her artist husband more than offset the slenderness of her dress allowance. There was a touch of *grande-dame* formality, a certain queenliness, in her manner of presiding which was in sharp contrast to the easy intimacy of the other three.

Helen Cash did not have this attraction of beauty. She was rather above the medium in all dimensions, but not in the least cumbersome. Her movements were a shade too precise to be gracious. But while she was not at all pretty, she caught and held attention. She was more of a person than Lillian. She had a real, if less obvious, appeal. She would have done very well as a model for a " Victory " or " The Spirit of the Republic." She had least charm at close quarters.

This was also true of her voice. It was a committee voice. It could read a report, cite statistics, state a policy with persuasive force. It sounded best from halfway back in a large hall, but it was a trifle overloud for intimate badinage.

In her world Helen was a great success. She was financial secretary — which means money raiser — of the National Association for Labor Legislation. She was one of the most highly paid women in social service work. She had "made good." Pete McGee had nicknamed her " Spot Cash."

Frank Lockwood did not dress like a genius, for Lillian insisted on a certain degree of neatness. Only his hair — which the winds had blown about too much for any reform — had escaped her control. His first love had been the sea, and New Ipswich, Maine, where he had spent his youth, where his ancestors had lived for generations, had left its mark on him. There was the gray of the misty northern sea in his eyes.

His eyes were what made every one love him.
People who had never heard his name were affected
by them. His eyes had done the trick for Win
Mathews, had pulled him out of the cultured shelter
of Boston Back Bay into a world of tense emotions
and stark realism. They had won the ill-tempered,
dishonest, drunken old woman who had been their
laundress, and changed her into a devoted slave.
They had drawn Lillian from another planet into a
strange, gypsy world where she could never be at home.

They were sad eyes, for they had seen beauty and
now had to look at other things. There was a picture
of his, "Moonlight on the Maine Sea," in the Corcoran at Washington, his portrait of Lillian in the
Metropolitan, and a mural piece in the Luxembourg.
A few years ago all the world of art critics were waiting eagerly for his next picture. But now he had a
contract as an illustrator at five thousand a year.
He was supporting his wife.

Pete McGee said he never could remember whether
Win was thirty-six or sixty-three — it depended on
which side of his face you were talking about. At
thirty, Win's hair in a one-sided way had begun to
turn gray. His left eyebrow now was almost white.
It had a bizarre effect, which arrested attention. It
seemed as if premature old age had brought an almost
flippant gaiety and sparkle to this side of his face,
while the other eye was plodding along in the pur-
suit of knowledge as a respectable eye should do.

Mathews' novels, all about the life of New York —
there was a string of six of them — were attracting
more and more readers. The first one had sold about

five thousand, the last one had reached twenty thousand, and his new one was running as a serial. He had none of the erratic temperament of his friend, Lockwood. Lillian would not have had any trouble with his hair; it was naturally orderly. The flame which burned within him was less brilliant than his friend's but more steady.

His manner was easy, almost too casual. He was so deeply interested in everybody else that he had no self-consciousness — and a certain self-consciousness is, after all, the basis of good manners. Most people found him hard to get acquainted with and, too easily discouraged, called him unresponsive or even rude. But those who persevered and reached through to intimacy found him every time better than when they had left him last.

From bills before the legislature in Albany, the discussion had come, with the dessert, to municipal politics. Lillian was bored. She was relieved when the meal was over and she could shift her guests into the parlor and superintend the placing of the coffee tray on an exquisite — but secondhand — directoire serving table.

"Frank," Helen said, for in spite of Lillian's striking beauty, these friends generally addressed themselves to her husband, "every time I see that coffee set, I fall more in love with it."

Lillian, busy with the pouring, did not follow the conversation. She was vexed with Helen for admiring these funny, old-fashioned, lusterware coffee things at this moment, for she was planning to persuade Frank to buy a new set more like her mother's.

At last her father's inventions had begun to make money and her parents were on the highroad to riches; they had moved to the Drive. Her mother had a solid silver coffee pot, gold-washed inside. She wondered if Helen's admiration of this lusterware would be so outspoken if she had known that Frank had bought it, almost for nothing, in a pawnshop.

This was the principal puzzle of life to her. Why did Frank and his friends value so many frayed, soiled, secondhand things? She liked things that were smart and new and costly. Many people who came to see her went into raptures over the little house, praising it because it was old. To her mind it was tiny, so inconspicuous, so almost shabby.

To be sure, the house had been thoroughly renovated at the time of her marriage, but this glorious restoration had not come to the district as a whole. A few neighboring houses had been redeemed by other artists, a few new tenements, dignified by the name of apartment houses, had been built, but nobody could pretend that it was a fashionable part of town. Although Frank and his friends liked the district, she wanted to move.

When she proposed it, Frank always asked an irrelevant question, about where in thunder had she hid his blue tie, or what were they going to have for dinner.

"My dear," he would say, when she insisted, as she always did, "we simply can't afford to move uptown on five thousand a year. Where did you say you'd put that tie?"

It was one of half a dozen subjects on which Frank

was adamant. She could not charm him, nor tease him, nor distress him into changing. While Lillian would admit quite freely to her mother, more guardedly to other married women, that Frank was not the perfectly docile husband, she had a proper pride which made her hide from any unmarried woman — Helen for instance — her dissatisfactions. She held her head high.

She sat in the stiff Gothic chair in which Frank had painted her. There were other chairs which she found more comfortable, but he had said that this one became her best and, uncertain of her own taste, she always trusted his. But being beautiful loses half its charm among people who are familiar with your beauty.

"If you people are through with politics," she broke in at the first opening, "I want to discuss Thanksgiving. We can't give up our annual picnic. Whom shall we invite?"

"Why, the same old crowd, of course," Helen said.

"We haven't got enough men, now that Pete has deserted."

"There's Lancaster and Frank and Win."

"But," Lillian insisted, "there are four of us girls."

"Of course, it's never sure about Eunice," Helen said. "She may not be up to a party."

"We must have her," Frank said emphatically, "if she's not feeling fit, we'll spend the day in the flat — or postpone the fiesta. We must have her. There's no hope of Pete?"

"No," Win groaned, with business of wiping away tears, "he's lashed to the mast."

"Isn't it fierce the way the old gang is breaking up," Frank said. "Remember how keen Mary always was on our sticking together! 'Just for a lapful of baby she left us; just for a husband to flaunt in our face.'"

"You started the stampede," Win remarked dryly.

"But, Win," Helen said, to steer out of dangerous waters, "you must know some men."

"Dozens of them, hundreds of them. But none who would quite fit. Thanksgiving Day should be a reunion of old pals. It's an unlucky day to make new acquaintances."

"You or Frank have got to find some one," Lillian said; "it don't much matter who. I've got a gorgeous idea. Generally we gave a theater party on Thanksgiving. But we ought to have some variety. Everything is Oriental these days. The Russian ballet — those plays, 'Mecca' and 'The Caliph's Daughter.' Let's make it a Persian supper. Let's have a contrast — fancy dress — an Arabian Nights' Entertainment on good old Puritan Thanksgiving Day!"

Win jumped up and snapped his fingers.

"I've an idea!"

"A man?"

"Yes. A regular man. He's Oriental enough. His name is Lane — Donald Lane — a queer chap. He has the apartment across the hall from our diggings. He's been there for six months or more. It's the old story — next door in New York is as far off as Patagonia. I've often passed him in the hallway, but we never spoke till recently.

"Weird people come to see him — Orientals — the way Russian refugees camp on Lancaster's door-step—— A few weeks ago I ran into him going down in the elevator; he had two of them with him — tall, gaunt men, with great turbans, white robes, flowing beards — talking some outlandish, guttural language. He put them in a taxi at the door. 'Who are your friends?' I asked. 'Moors,' he said — just like that — without any explanation, as though it were the simplest thing in the world. We walked over to Broadway together. He told me that he was the secretary of some Oriental society.

"After that I kept an eye on him. There's a young fellow living with him. He wears ordinary clothes and a red fez — a Turk, I imagine. About a month ago I came home late one night — Pete was up at Albany — and was greeted by the strangest music I ever heard — weird but beautiful. I could not guess the instrument. At first it sounded like a flute, but there were some full cello notes and now and then a heart-piercing, high, violin note. It sounded just outside my window.

"I tiptoed across the room and looked out — the queerest sight this little old New York ever produced! This chap, Lane, was sitting cross-legged on the fire escape, staring up at the faintest new moon, working a barbaric fiddle. There was a round drumhead, like a banjo, and a short neck. Instead of strings there was a wisp of horsehair; he fingered this and sawed across it with a bow of one string. It was just the reverse of our violin. And even as

I watched him, I would have sworn that some of the notes came from a reed.

"When he saw me he was mightily embarrassed — hoped his noise had not disturbed me. I crawled out on the balcony and looked at the instrument. It was a beautiful piece of craftsmanship, all chased with elaborate arabesques and inlaid with gold and ivory. He told me its name, which begins with three r's and ends with three b's — with hardly any vowels in between. I asked him what tune he was playing and he said it wasn't a tune, just something he made up as he went along. 'It's the first beautiful night I've seen in New York. The moon makes the buildings across the Square look a little like mountains,' he said, by way of explanation — as if that were sufficient excuse for sitting out on the fire escape and serenading the moon on an inverted, heathen fiddle!

"I asked him where his home was, and he seemed surprised. Apparently the idea of having a home had never occurred to him. So I asked some questions about music, and he opened up at once and invited me inside his window. Oriental music and poetry seem to be his specialty. He did not talk much about himself, but I gathered that he had traveled all over the East. He spoke familiarly of Samarkand, Ispahan, Cashmere, and places like that.

"At last I put my foot in it by saying that I liked the Rubaiyat. He flared up at that. Omar, it seems, was a lightweight — a minor poet among the Persians. And Fitzgerald, he said, had mistranslated him shamefully. The quatrain about 'Man's forgiveness ask — and take' offended him most. 'Not even a wine drinker like Omar,' he said, ' would have written such a blasphemy.' He seemed to think that any one who liked the Rubaiyat was a lowbrow — hardly worth talking to.

"I did not see him again for some time, but a few days ago he suddenly forgave my literary tastes, knocked at my door, and asked if I liked Turkish cigarettes. He gave me a handful — the best I've ever smoked. He said a friend of his makes them, and I ordered a couple of hundred. They're unbelievably cheap — I'll send you some.

"I don't know anything about him, except what I've told you. He's a queer one. But he's intelligent, really erudite, I judge, in his specialty. He's painfully shy — seems to want to be friendly and not quite certain how it's done. I guess he's a solitary chap — unused to company. I don't suppose that he'd fit in very well — generally — probably knows nothing and cares less about the things we're keen on. But if Lillian wants an Oriental spread, he might help.

"I tell you what. Come to breakfast Sunday. We haven't had one of our old-fashioned, Sunday breakfasts since Pete fell by the wayside. I'll invite Lane, and you can all look him over. If he passes the examination, Lillian can ask him to dinner and get acquainted. Yes? No?"

After a little more discussion and repeated assurances from Win that this was all he knew about the Stranger, they played a few rubbers of bridge.

After eleven the party broke up, and Win walked home with Helen.

"It's funny about Lillian," she said, "I haven't sized her up yet. Still — after all these years — she seems an outsider. It startles me when she says 'us girls.' Somehow I never think of her as one of 'us.'"

"She never will be," Win said bitterly.

"I wonder why I don't like her more. She's so beautiful! Every time I see her, I'm surprised again — she's breath-taking."

"Oh, Frank arranges that. He's stage manager. If he didn't design her clothes, she'd look like a chorus girl."

"Come, come!" Helen laughed. "She *is* beautiful. You must admit that, even if you don't like her."

"Well, perhaps she is — but I dislike her just the same. I know it's jealousy — of course, I'm jealous. Ten years and more Frank and I chummed together, then she butted in. And besides, it rumples up my aura to hear her say, 'It don't' and 'I have got.'"

"Frank seems contented."

"What's that to do with it?" Win demanded savagely. "What's happiness compared to what he's given up? He wasn't only *a* painter, he was *the* painter — the pure essence — and now he's an illustrator! What's happiness — a pretty wife to kiss — compared with the place he held — and the promise? He used to be a rare soul and now he's a meal ticket! It's a crime! And besides I'm not so sure that he is happy."

They had come to the door of Helen's apartment.

"You ought to know better than to start me thinking about Lillian at this time of night," Win growled. "Now I'll go to bed with a grouch."

"Well, to change the subject, how about this Stranger? You think we'll like him?"

"I don't take any responsibility. It's up to you people to decide. I said Thanksgiving is an unlucky day to make new acquaintances."

"We'll see," Helen said. "He sounds interesting. I'm curious about him. Good night."

"Good night," Win called back from the sidewalk, as Helen let herself in with her latchkey. "Love to Eunice. Tell her I'll expect her Sunday morning. We'll need her advice about this Stranger."

CHAPTER II

EUNICE BENDER

There was a silent and mysterious tragedy back of Eunice Bender. Nature had condemned her mother's stock — the Ripley family was dying out. It was a strange matter, for they had always held an honored place among their neighbors; their passing, one by one, had been mourned by the whole community. We would expect nature to cherish a breed so generally beloved. But at some time, in some unknown way, some obscure law of life had been violated. The verdict was plain.

Eunice's mother and her sister, Mrs. Clarkeson, were the only two of that generation — and it had been a large family — who had grown to maturity. Mrs. Bender had died in childbirth, and Mrs. Clarkeson had not entirely escaped the family sentence, for she and her large brood of children were " sickly."

Eunice's memories of her father were slight, for he had been killed in a railroad accident when she was five, and even before that she had been taken into the Clarkeson family. Her uncle, Mr. Clarkeson, was town clerk and had no further ambitions nor aptitudes, so her small income from the insurance money not only had to meet her own expenses, but also helped to pay his chronic debts. In this cheerless atmosphere Eunice had grown up.

As no one had expected her to live so long, she had had no formal education. Being always considered too frail to do anything, they had left her free to do what she pleased. And the thing which had pleased her most was to draw pictures of her young cousins. To persuade them to sit still, while she sketched them, she told them stories, which often, half unconsciously, twisted themselves into rhythm and rhyme.

Even in this hobby of drawing, she had no instruction — there were no teachers of such things in the village of West Newleigh. There were not even any noteworthy pictures to learn from. The half tones in the magazines were her only approach to art. So often too weak to be about, never strong enough for a scramble in the woods, she had not even been able to come to close quarters with the beauty of nature. The flowers in the Clarkesons' yard were few and scraggly. They kept chickens. And the children preferred cats to wild birds.

The one bright spot in this dismal existence was Helen Cash. Her parents lived next door, and the two girls had been friends from earliest childhood. But chronic invalidism had kept Eunice at home, when Helen fared forth to school.

Helen's college had been near by. She lived at home, going to her classes by trolley, and so was able to "look in" on Eunice every day. It was not any motive of good works, of "visiting the sick and in prison," which brought her. She liked Eunice. Too healthy herself ever to take note of it, she found a strange appeal in her friend's weakness. The Clarkeson family was shiftless, and the house, overfull of children, was none too orderly. But somehow Eunice's room was always bright — a place to which it was a privilege to come.

We carry with us type pictures of those we love, composites of all our memories, in which only the salient and significant things stand out. Sometimes, of course, Eunice would be up and about, but in Helen's picture she was always in her narrow white bed. There was as motif an orchidlike fragility, an other-worldly loveliness, and for dominants, the haunting beauty of great eyes and two amazing braids of golden hair — hair that Melisande would have envied.

Generally, when Helen "looked in," the children were about, and Eunice's fine, long hands were busy cutting out paper dolls for them or drawing pictures to illustrate the story she was telling. The youngsters always disappeared when Helen came. It was for this, more than anything else, that she pitied Eunice — having to spend so much time with children.

When they had gone, Eunice would turn to Helen those great eyes inquiringly. There were always questions in them: "How does it feel to be really alive?" "What is the world outside like?" And Helen, seated on the foot of the bed, would tell her all about life. At the age of ten, she had explained the universe to Eunice from the point of view of the West Newleigh Grammar School. After she went to college, her discourses took on a more academic tone. But always — even at ten — Helen had been quite sure of her judgments, and it had never occurred to Eunice to question them.

So, although her outlook on life was limited, Eunice knew Helen's life with unusual intimacy. She was ever an approving audience, which made it easy for Helen to talk, to recount all her adventures, to tell — everything.

Eunice had heard in detail of the tribulations of freshmen. She had been told how the dogmatic religion of the village Sunday school had come to grief under scrutiny from the scientific point of view. She had been told about the men who danced with Helen, and those who wanted to go on dancing. Helen had been proposed to twice and had confided all the details. Eunice had learned a very precise and vigorous formula of refusal. She had also read the despairing letters of the rejected suitors.

Eunice had much time to read, in the long evenings after the children were a-bed, and she had studied all of Helen's textbooks, had played, not unsuccessfully, with her examination papers. As she had to puzzle her way through all this without a teacher, some of this long-distance education sank into her mind more durably than into Helen's.

Above all, she had learned from Helen a familiarity with the modern feminist attitude toward life. Helen would have to earn her living when she finished college. Her father was the village doctor, the Pennsylvanian countryside was healthy, and there were other children to educate. Helen, far from being dejected by this prospect, gloried in it. She believed in the " economic independence of women."

Mrs. Cash had planned that Helen should teach in the village high school, but Helen had other plans.

"I won't stay in West Newleigh," she said to Eunice, "teaching things that bore me, to children who aren't interested — waiting for some man to marry me! No, I want to do something worth while."

Merely "earning a living" was too meager a goal for her ambitions. She wanted to do it largely and splendidly, not only for herself and her own comfort, but also as a demonstration — on behalf of womanhood. The field of activity which she had chosen for herself was "Social Service," what an earlier generation called "Philanthropy." "Municipal Housekeeping" and phrases from Mrs. Gilman's "Woman and Economics" were always on her lips. Here were large opportunities for women. "It's a new frontier," she told Eunice; "there is a demand for social pioneers."

In the Easter vacation of her senior year, Helen went on a voyage of adventure to New York, and she brought back to Eunice the great news that she had found a job. It was an investigation into the uses and abuses of employment agencies. She was to begin work as soon as she left college and she was to live in a settlement on Second Avenue.

Eunice was in bed, when Helen brought this news. She had expected it. Helen wanted to go and Helen always got her way. Eunice knew how marvelous the opening seemed to her friend. Of course she was glad about it, and yet —— She had to clinch her hands very tightly under the bedclothes not to spoil Helen's joy by letting her see how gloomy and very lonely life would be in West Newleigh without her.

"Tell me about New York," she said to avoid the unpleasant thought.

"Oh, Eunice, I can't — it's too wonderful! The women in the Settlement are real people — modern. Every one hard at work at something that counts. I had a long talk with Mrs. Gilman; she's every bit as good as her books. She fixed up this job for me. It'll be a stepping-stone to other work — better and more worth-while. There are a dozen girls at the Settlement, all interesting. The ones I liked best were Irene Penton and Mary Dutton, a kindergartner and a trained nurse. They're only a few years older than I, but already they've made a reputation for themselves. Between them, they've cut down the rate of infant mortality in the district — so that everybody is talking about it. Doctors come from all over — even from Europe — to study their methods. Now they're working for a maternity hospital. It must be wonderful to do things like that — to be somebody. They're individuals. They have real lives — personalities of their own.

"The men they introduced me to are just as fine. All of them have some real achievements to their credit. There is an artist, Frank Lockwood, who — they say — is very good. And a novelist, who lives with him, Winslow Mathews. I've brought down one of his books for you to read. It's about a Settlement — a good story. I liked him very much. Then there's a professor of ethnology, from Columbia, Lancaster. I did not see much of him, but they say he's awfully clever. And a funny Irishman named McGee.

He's always laughing and joking, but they all think highly of him. I didn't quite understand what he does — it's something in connection with the legislature in Albany.

"The finest thing is the way the men treat the women — as equals, comrades. No silly flirting. They're not solemn; they're serious. You see they're all hard at work — on something important, something that counts. They're the kind of people I want for my friends. And now I've the chance to live with them, to work with them. It's perfectly wonderful. My dream's come true."

For an hour or more she sat there on the foot of Eunice's bed, telling about these new friends, about her new work. The rush of her talk, hot, hastily phrased pictures of the city, quick, incisive descriptions of people, bewildered Eunice. How fatiguing it must be, she thought, to be really alive, to have such thrilling experiences.

And Helen's recital, was thrilling, for there is a note more stirring than that of triumph — it was all about glorious beginnings. There is always, something poignant and moving in the hopes of starting out. The Song of Victory is never so thrilling as "Le chant du départ." And Helen's talk of New York was a pæan to battles yet to win.

So life had led Eunice — drearily — through a quarter of a century. The only high lights had been furnished by this friend, who had advantage. Helen was a forth-faring person utterly undaunted, and Eunice attributed these qualities to health. It had never occurred to her that a well person might be

a coward. "Courage" and "health" she thought
meant the same thing. And so she could not think
of herself, so pitifully ill, as heroic. But the Great
God Himself, if He took notice, must have admired,
almost envied, her courage as she faced this new
misery of loneliness after Helen's departure. The
long, monotonous days and nights were so dismally
uniform that even the occasional spells of pain were
a relief. "Oh, I'll write — often," Helen had said;
"of course, I'll write all about it." So the postman
became the great personage in Eunice's life.

But from the very first, Helen's letters were irregular — there was such a swirl of things to do in
New York! It had been so much easier to "look in"
than it was to find time to write. One week there
was only a postcard, with a picture of Brooklyn
Bridge and a penciled line, "Too rushed to write."

Helen did her best to keep up the correspondence.
Now and then something, which less valiant people
might have called "homesickness," overtook her and
she wrote at length to Eunice. In this manner the
stay-at-home became acquainted with Helen's work
and her new friends.

There was a long letter about the maternity hospital. It was to be the keystone in the arch which
Helen's two best friends were building. Frank Lockwood had drawn some "stunning" posters for it.
Win Mathews had "handled the publicity." Pete
McGee had pulled wires till the Board of Estimate
had apportioned some city funds for its upkeep.
And there was a great deal about how Helen, over
and above her regular job, which she described

as "very easy," helped to raise money for the building.

"Raising money," it soon developed, was Helen's forte. When the Investigation of Employment Agencies was finished, she became financial secretary for a "Deaf and Dumb Asylum," which had fallen into a rut and was being outstripped in the scramble for alms by newer and brisker organizations. She wrote a good deal about this job.

"It's the first really important work I've had; it gives me a chance." She mailed Eunice some of the "literature" she was sending out, and told in detail of the expedients and maneuvers by which she drew renewed attention to this neglected institution. "It's queer. The Charity Organization Society has done a lot to work out efficient methods to distribute relief, but as far as I can see, nobody has used much brains on raising money. Most of the charities stick to the old-fashioned practice of sending out printed or mimeographed — impersonal — circulars to a big mailing list on the chance that one out of ten will bring in a small check. Eighty per cent. of the income of this asylum came in driblets of five or ten dollars. I believe in direct personal appeals; it's a lot more efficient. There are a great many rich people who suffer from deafness — I go after them. Already, I've brought in twenty checks for five hundred and two for a thousand. Everybody seems surprised, but it's only common sense."

Once every year Helen came home for Christmas, and these were red-letter occasions for Eunice. "There are so many things," Helen said, "that it's hard to write about." One of these subjects was Pete McGee. His name had occurred frequently in her letters, especially after she had left the Deaf and Dumb Asylum for work with the Child Labor Committee, in which he also was interested. This new work threw them constantly together. At first, Helen had been enthusiastic about him, but in a letter a few weeks before one of her visits home, she had written that he had proposed to her. She had given no details and her only comment was " I'm sick about it."

"Yes," she said, when Eunice brought up the subject, "it did make me sick. I'd put him on such a high plane. He's not clever like Win, nor so intellectual as Lancaster; but in so many ways he's more effective than either of them — he gets things done! I like him — a lot! And now he goes and spoils everything by trying to make love to me — just like an ordinary man.

"Of course I stopped him as soon as I understood, but he's always joking and it's hard to know when he's in earnest. I really was surprised — and not a bit pleased. It was so fine working together, a frank, free friendship — never thinking about such things. Now, I'll always have to be on my guard. How I hate it!"

In this secondhand acquaintance, Eunice had been most interested in the artist, Frank Lockwood; she wanted most to hear about him.

"Everybody likes Frank," Helen said, "more, I guess, than I do. They say he's a wonderful painter, but it all seems sort 'of ineffectual to me. I wish I knew more about such things. 'Art' seems to me so indefinite, so hard to value. The others think it is very important, but I can't see that it gets anywhere. I can't find any standard to judge it by. People rave over one picture and despise another and I don't understand why. I suppose I haven't any taste. But Frank must be clever, people who pretend to know say he's a genius. He's won a lot of prizes. His last one — Win says it's his best — was bought by a banker named Baldwin. He has done some amusing Mother Goose decorations for the Kindergarten, and now he's working on some friezes for the auditorium of the Settlement.

"I like him — nobody could help liking him — but I don't understand him. He seems way up in the air — not interested in real things. And the girls say that he used to drink — horribly. But he's always sober now."

A letter written a few weeks after Helen's return to the city was devoted to Win. "He's interested in art, too, in literature. He lives with Frank in the Studio on the Square, not far from the Settlement. He writes well. I'm sending you an article of his about the street-car strike. It's real, it will help the men a lot. I wish he'd stick to this sort of work. It's something concrete and useful — more so, I think, than his novels. They're clever and entertaining, but somehow they seem to me — well, less *real*. He's a little like Frank. I don't mean that he drinks too much, not that way, but now and then he seems absent-minded — sort of gazing off into space."

Eunice, propped up on her pillows, often "gazed

off into space." There was a very wonderful make-believe land beyond the four walls of her little room, where everybody was strong and healthy. It did not seem to her a very heinous fault. She tried to say this in her answer, but Helen retorted sharply.

"I haven't time to gaze off into space. I don't see how any serious, active person can. This is a real world we live in and so much of it needs to be put right. Why waste time in idle, abstracted contemplation? Just as one example — Irene and Mary have decreased the number of babies who die out of every hundred born in this district. Think what infant mortality means! All the pain and energy and expenses of childbirth wasted — sheer waste! Gazing off into space won't help. If the nation really got down to the job and did everywhere what these two girls have done here in this district, we could save thousands and thousands of babies. But this sort of thing means work — not dreams.

"There are so many ways of concrete usefulness, how can people find time to paint pictures or write novels — gaze off into space? Art won't keep the babies from dying. I like Frank and Win, but I've more respect for Pete — in spite of his laughing ways, he's always on the job, getting things done — real things."

In another letter, Helen wrote of Professor Lancaster. "The rest of us call each other by our first names just naturally, but somehow nobody does him. He's always 'Lancaster.' He's a bit stiff and formal. He comes from Oregon, but he looks like a New Englander — more than either Frank or Win. He's

rather like St. Gaudens' statue of the Puritan. He's
the type you respect long before you begin to like
him. He's an immensely hard worker, way up at the
top of his specialty — *the* authority on American
Indians. He's a very earnest Socialist and has swung
us all into the party except Pete.

"They're a queer pair, living together in an apartment they call 'The Diggings' across the Square
from the studio — not agreeing on anything except
to like each other.

"Pete is always poking fun at him; says he's so
used to hard work that, when he has nothing to do, he
does it intensely. He's also secretary of the Society
of Friends of Russian Freedom — very much interested in the revolutionary movement over there and
in the Russian comrades here in New York. One
night Pete came home from Albany on the midnight
train and found three Russian refugees sleeping in
his bed! Another time, Pete's mother, a very precise
and formal old lady, came to town and wanted to see
her son's rooms. Pete picked her up at her hotel
and took her to 'The Diggings.' When he opened
the door, his mother was nearly scared out of her
life. Lancaster had some Hopi Indians from a Wild
West Show — he'd been adopted into their tribe —
and he'd brought them to his room to do a snake dance
for him. He was catching their songs in a phono-
graph."

More than once, Helen reverted to Pete's unrea-
sonableness. "I've explained to him a dozen times,"
she wrote, "that I don't want to get married. It isn't
that I'm refusing to marry *him*, I'm refusing matri-

mony in the abstract. I simply can't consider it *now*. This love business is just like writing poetry — I haven't time. I'm too busy. There's too much to do.

"I'm hurt at him — very much hurt — always spoiling things this way. It isn't as if he were a stranger, who didn't understand how I feel about it. He knows. We've talked it over a hundred times; I don't want *to stop work* to get married. It's not merely personal ambition — not just to make a name for myself. It's much broader than that.

"We women simply must struggle for our place in the world — for recognition. Here I am just beginning. I've made a good start, but I've just begun and it isn't an easy job I've undertaken. I'm building up a new profession, I'm creating a job. A social-service financier — that's what Pete calls me himself. It isn't any special cleverness of mine that's succeeding, but steady, hard work — grinding. I want to become an expert at it and now I'm learning the job.

"It would all be wasted — everything I've learned, all the work I've done — if I should stop now. Perhaps after a while — some time in the future — perhaps. But now, I simply can't think of getting married.

"Men are queer about this feminism. Pete has done a lot of work for suffrage, but he forgets all about the ideal — is quite willing to mix up all my plans — just because he happens to fall in love. It seems to me appallingly selfish.

"We're all distressed about Mary. She's decided to get married and leave us. The man's all right, he was house surgeon in the maternity hospital at first and we liked him. He's gone abroad now for a year's postgraduate work in Vienna and is coming back to start practice out in California. It's an awful blow to us all — especially to Irene. They were such a strong team, working together — but Mary says she wants babies of her own. It's tragic — this continual struggle between personal happiness and the public welfare — the Home vs. the Commonwealth.

> "'God bless me and my wife,
> My son John and his wife,
> Us four,
> No more.'

"That's what starting a home means. All Mary's special training and experience, all her valuable and unique talents, in the infant mortality work must go by the board. It seems to me like a desertion. Pete feels just the same about Mary as I do, but that doesn't stop him from trying to pry me loose from my job."

So from these infrequent visits and irregular letters Eunice got news of the world beyond West Newleigh. To be sure it was a very small sector of the great world on which Helen reported, but it seemed very wonderful to Eunice — a world of youth and health, of ardent hopes and noble efforts.

Her one escape from the all-pervading gloom of the Clarkeson household was a rustic bench under a great elm tree beyond the village. On her "good days," when she was able to be up, she always walked there. The beauty of her view was the one treasure of her youth, and in a way it was a private treasure, for no one used this bench except lovers after nightfall. Her neighbors did not care much for scenery, but Eunice loved the place.

West Newleigh, in itself unlovely, sat on the crest of a rolling hill in eastern Pennsylvania. There was a broad outlook from this seat, across a gentle valley, ten miles to the next ridge and the horizon beyond was the purple gray of higher hills. The view held no indication of its date. It might have been the English countryside in the days when the good king Alfred was driving out the Danes. Much of the Danube country, through which the Crusaders marched on their way to the Holy Sepulchre, must have looked very like this bit of modern Pennsylvania.

It was here that Eunice read and reread Helen's letters. It was here that she brought the books and pamphlets Helen sent. She read with care — and much perplexity — the books on Socialism. She was relieved to find that they had nothing in them about bomb-throwing, but — knowing no other life than that of her simple village, they had little meaning for her.

She could not have understood them, and the reports of investigations and so forth, which Helen sent at all if it had not been for Win's novels. He visualized and made alive the people tabulated in the statistics, and also the people who gathered them.

"The Six Hundred" was the one of his books she liked best. Again and again she had read the opening paragraphs.

"The race," he had written, "is rather like an onion: so many layers fitting tightly about the next smaller one — layer after layer down to the tiny germ in the middle. Within the race are scores of great nations, within each nation, provinces; they in turn divided and subdivided into counties, townships, neighborhoods — families. And of course each one of us is the central kernel of his own universe.

"This concentric grouping is not only geographic. We live not only in 'our street,' 'our town,' 'our country,' but also in 'our religious belief,' 'our political creed,' perhaps most of all in 'our trade.'

"Few of these circles within circles are more interesting, more worthy of study, than the social workers. They inhabit no fixed frontiers. Theirs is a fellowship, not of territorial chance, but of common aspirations. There is some mystic magnetism which draws to New York at some time in their career, almost every one who has a passion to make this old world of ours a cleaner, more wholesome, and happier place.

"Very few of these social workers are New York born. They come as often from Kansas or the Coast as from the thirteen original States. A surprising number of them, including the calmest and the most fervid, come from Chicago. In the Charities Building you can hear the accent of every State. But no matter where they were born, no matter what twang or burr sticks to their tongues, they are intensely New Yorkers.

"They are the city become self-conscious. They have investigated the East Side and the West Side. They understand the transportation problems of Brooklyn. They know all the police captains of the Bronx, which ones are honest and which ones intend to get rich. If you chance to be interested in the violations of the tenement-house law in Queens, or the percentage of wayward girls in the city institutions of the Borough of Richmond who are feeble-minded, you can find one of these social workers, who has written a doctor's thesis on the subject.

"No matter what you are seeking among them, you will find youth. Reverence for things old, for retrospection, is at a discount among them. They never produced but one historian —

and he proposed a new philosophy of history. The principal preoccupation of this group is the unborn future.

"If you make inquiries, you will find many people — socially successful people — who never heard of these social workers. I have called them 'The Six Hundred' because of their high daring, but it also serves to distinguish them from the better advertised 'Four Hundred,' who live uptown. They are not fashionable. Other people — prosperous people, with a vested interest in things as they are — will tell you that these social workers are freaks, trouble makers, agitators — nuisances.

"There is a fable yet to be written on what the lump of dough thought about the cake of yeast. Some of the dough probably cut the yeast socially and ignored it, while some of the dough undoubtedly objected to radical innovation and edited weekly journals which advocated the suppression of yeast. These social workers are a ferment. They are rejuvenating all the implications of our city life and they are beginning to be interested in rural problems. Whether the dough likes it or not, it can not resist the leavening.

"So if you wish to know what New York City and the broad continent behind it will be like fifty years hence, go to these people. Do not pay attention to what the 'best people' say about them, do not let your attention be distracted by the queer clothes they sometimes wear, nor by the vile food they often eat in their garrets, but study their dreams.

"Nothing much matters to them but their dreams — and bitter hard work to make them come true."

Eunice would close her eyes very tightly, when she read such things. She did not like to cry, but the tears always tried to come through when she let herself imagine too vividly what life might be like for her, if only she were well. From Helen and her books she had acquired a "social conscience." She would have liked to be a part of this rejuvenating ferment, to bear her share in bringing the New Day.

When she " gazed off into space," through the walls
of her little bedroom or from her seat under the elm,
the make-believe stage and beyond was not set to
represent the glory that was Greece, nor the grandeur
that was Rome. She daydreamed, not of levees at the
Court of St. James nor of dinners at Sherry's, but of
walking beside Helen in the great city, of the brave
plans and earnest efforts of her friends in the real
world.

It was not often that Eunice could get to this favorite spot; once or twice a week in summertime. · The
short walk was always a great event for her, but it
did her more good than any medicine — just to sit
there an hour or so in silence and read and dream.

Many a languid hour, when she was bed-bound, was
cheered for her by her small cousins. On account .
of their mother's ill health, they would have been decidedly neglected children if Eunice had not fulfilled
the duties of a nursery governess. But it did not
seem an unpleasant task to her; she loved children,
and, besides, any rôle was better than absolute use-
lessness. The Fates had been unkind to her in not
letting her know how the wild flowers grow on the
hillside. But she knew just how a nose grows on a
little boy's face.

CHAPTER III

EUNICE AND THE CITY

Four years had passed thus monotonously for Eunice, since Helen had left on her quest for things "worth while," when a new burden was laid on her frail shoulders — poverty.

Mr. Clarkeson, her uncle, a tall, gaunt, strangely ineffectual man, came into her bedroom one morning with an air of solemnity and harassed depression. He habitually looked on the bright side of things, but this morning the sun of his optimism was eclipsed. With much embarrassment and many digressions after meaningless details, he explained that an unfortunate investment had wiped out all that was left of the Ripley heritage and Eunice's insurance money as well. There was nothing left for them all but his small and inadequate salary as town clerk. He was very anxious to have her understand that it had been "a perfectly sound investment." Had he cared for his wife's money and hers these many years and never lost a cent? This showed that he was safe and sane.

For the details of the catastrophe Eunice had no comprehension nor interest; the ruin was all she understood. What to do without a cent in the world? She could not live at her uncle's expense; he was going to have a miserably close time with his own family. She had never been of much use to any one and now

she threatened to be a burden.   The weakness and the
pain with which she was so familiar seemed a very
small thing to bear compared to this.

The first glimmer of hope that penetrated her bewildered dismay was the possibility of selling some
of her pictures to a magazine.   Years before she had
sent one of her drawings to a juvenile competition in
The Children's World and had won a prize of five
dollars and a life's subscription.   Nowadays, as she
showed the magazine to the children, she often
thought that her pictures were just as good.   In spite
of her cloistered life, she was wise enough to realize
that grown-ups will pay almost anything to keep
children quiet.

Without taking any one into her confidence, she
mailed to the magazine a colored drawing she had
made of a circus parade.   The principal figure was
a wonderful giraffe, which would have shocked any
naturalist, but was exactly what her cousins thought
a proper giraffe should look like.   Accompanying it,
she sent a rhymed story for the picture to illustrate.

The next weeks were breathless for her, thrilling
and miserable.   At best she hoped for five or ten dollars, and the family bills were running up appallingly.
At last the picture came back, but there was a friendly,
encouraging letter from Mr. Britton, the editor.   He
said that he liked the verse, but that the colors she
had used in the picture made reproduction impossibly
expensive.   "You are evidently unfamiliar with the
processes we employ, with the limitations of the press
and of printer's ink.   I am sending you herewith a
copy of 'Picture Printing,' which we have compiled

for the benefit of our contributors. *The Children's World* makes a specialty of developing new talent. Your picture is unavailable, but, if you will redraw it in accordance with the instructions in this book, we may be able to use it."

Eunice found the book hopeless. She did not know the difference between half-tone screens and the three-color process. It was too complicated — too scientific — to understand. She tried embroidery. But in four weeks, the Women's Exchange sold only one dollar's worth of her work and she had a sick suspicion that the rector's wife had bought that out of kindness. She had some fine old lace, which had come to her through at least three generations and she sold a hundred dollars' worth of that to a curio shop in Philadelphia for twenty-five.

She did not write to Helen about this new " trouble." Why should she? There was nothing Helen could do about it. And so, having no one to confide in, her despair was all the darker.

Two days after she had written to the State Board of Charities to learn the terms of admission to the poor house, she received a " follow-up letter " from the editor of *The Children's World*. Mr. Britton had been impressed by that strange giraffe, his own children had been enthusiastic, and, what was more impressive, they had liked the verses. Now, although it is the adults who pay the subscription, it is desirable to have something in a children's magazine which will interest children, and the contributors who can write the kind of verses the children really like, instead of the kind that their parents think it would be nice for them to like, are hard to find. A letter of encouragement would cost Mr. Britton only a postage stamp and there was a chance that if this unknown Miss Bender worked hard — at no expense to him — she might learn how to make a good deal of money for him.

The letter produced the effect he had hoped for, it was just the fillip her fainting courage needed. It came on one of her "good days" and she walked down to the village printing shop to look at a press. There was a new foreman, who, in soberer days, had been a photo-engraver. He was quite willing to stop work and talk. With his help and the book to guide her, she set to work again.

This new effort was rewarded by a check for fifty dollars. Of course Eunice was elated — a check like that now and then would more than pay her expenses. A second picture was soon mailed and accepted.

Just as Eunice had been reluctant to tell Helen of her misfortune, she was too modest to write of her good luck. Her uncle, who was hurt in his manly pride at being rescued by his invalid niece, was discouraging. It was one of the few things about which he was pessimistic. He warned her not to expect too much, they would soon tire of her foolish pictures. It is often easier to see the silver lining to one's own failures than to another's successes.

Of course Eunice quickly developed an ambition. She started work on a series — "The Adventures of Tit, Tat, Toe, and Little Tot." They were aged five, four, three and one. Except for their size they looked exactly alike. They all wore white Russian blouses and broad black belts and wore their hair à la Jeanne d'Arc. The three older children had a nurse named Hattie, who was very tall and thin. Little Tot lived in a baby carriage, pushed by a very fat nurse named Mattie, and trailed along behind. In one picture they shot off firecrackers on the Fourth. In another they celebrated Tot's first birthday with a lawn party. In the third they went to the barnyard to watch the milking. Tat had always thought that cream came from calves, just as milk comes from cows. Tit, being a boy and so much older, knew better and pointed the finger of scorn at her.

Eunice thought that fifty dollars was a generous pay for her work — Mr. Britton had said so — and it would not have occurred to her to ask for more, but just as she was finishing the third of this series, before she had sent in any of them, a letter came to her from *Toyland* offering her a hundred dollars for a contribution. She inclosed this letter to Mr. Britton, when she sent the first three of her series to him as samples. There was a very quick response from him inclosing a contract for a year's exclusive work in *The Children's World* — twelve of the "Tit, Tat, Toe, and Little Tot" pictures and verses, at a hundred and fifty a month.

That was more than her uncle earned! She wrote about it in her next letter to Helen —"I'm doing some drawings and verses for *The Children's World*. It's easy because I've always done it for fun. They pay well, which is very lucky, for Uncle Tom lost some money on a bad investment and now I can help them a little." This letter reached Helen when she

was off on a trip, organizing child labor committees
in the up-State towns. She tried once or twice to
buy a copy of *The Children's World,* but was not able
to find one and, before she returned to New York, she
had forgotten the matter. Eunice did not allude to
it again. Of course she felt herself wonderfully fortunate; but, after all, drawing pictures for children
is petty business compared to the " real," " worth-
while " work that Helen was doing.

When " The Adventures of Tit, Tat, Toe, and Little
Tot " began to appear in *The Children's World,* Mr.
Britton congratulated himself on his acumen. In
Eunice he had discovered a gold mine. The pictures
had " caught on." He decided that there would be a
rich by-product in the publication of this series as
a Christmas book, and — without realizing what an
upheaval he was causing in her life — asked her to
come to New York to discuss the matter.

What a blaze this request lit in Eunice's brain!
She was not much interested in the book, but she had
always wanted to visit New York. She had never permitted herself to realize how much she wanted to see
Helen's friends, the Settlement, the Maternity Hospital — above all she wanted to see Frank's pictures.
But all this had seemed impractical. She could not
afford the expense and, besides, she had no excuse for
going; she would only be in the way, interfering with
busy people. But now, she had business of her
own.

And for the first time in her life she felt well enough
to go. The thought that she had something to do,
some regular work, some usefulness in the world, had

been the best of tonics for her. In the years before, she had often stayed in bed, because there was no reason to get up, but most of these pictures she was drawing were set out of doors and so, wanting to be up, she found it easier than she had thought and every day that she did get up made it easier the next.

This momentous letter reached her on a Friday. For the first time in her life she looked up a railroad time-table. She wrote, in a great flutter of excitement, a formal letter to Mr. Britton, saying that she would call at his office at ten on Monday morning. She wrote at length to Helen, carefully explaining that business of her own was bringing her to town and that she did not intend to be a bother. It was only at the very first that she would need any help, advice about a hotel and so forth. But she did hope that Helen could meet her train.

It was a decidedly frayed young person who got off the sleeping car in Jersey City on Monday morning. In spite of the lethargic name of her conveyance, Eunice had not closed an eye all night. And trouble began for her at once — she had not counted on having to cross the ferry alone. It was a rather breath-taking adventure, but it was soon forgotten in the blank dismay of not finding Helen to welcome her on the Manhattan side.

Eunice was very bewildered as she stood there alone in the ferry house. The city had taken on a forbidding and unfriendly aspect. She had expected that Helen would meet her and take her to the Settlement to stay — but she could not go there uninvited. The only place she could think of to go was the Hotel

Santa Fé, of which Helen had spoken. It was at least near the Settlement. She gritted her teeth and found a cab.

Why had Helen failed her? This question troubled her so much that she hardly noticed the city, which she had so often tried to imagine. The roar of an "elevated" overhead startled her into attention for a minute, but through most of the ride she was only vaguely conscious of the rumble and jar, of the feverish hurly-burly life of the streets.

After a forlorn and very lonely breakfast — between every unappetizing mouthful of which she asked herself what could be the matter with Helen — she resolved to telephone to the Settlement and find out. The young lady at the other end of the line gave up what information she had reluctantly. Miss Cash was out of town. She had been away for a week. She was attending a Senate hearing at Albany on the Child Labor Law. She had not left word when she would be back. Even more reluctantly she consented to take a message for Miss Cash that Miss Bender was stopping at the Santa Fé.

It was a great relief to Eunice to learn that Helen had been out of town and so could not have received her letter. This was a very much more comforting explanation of her lack of welcome than the thought of indifference or displeasure at her coming. But what a fool she had been not to wait till she was sure that Helen was in town. She had counted more than she had realized on her friend. Now, she would have to do everything herself — alone. This was dismaying — but dismay would not get her anywhere, so she stiffened her upper lip and set out bravely to the office of *The Children's World*.

The memory of that first interview with Mr. Britton always caused Eunice a shudder. It was her first face-to-face encounter with business. In spite of her inexperience in such matters, she realized that however fine a gentleman Mr. Britton might be — and he had a very impressive office — it was all a matter of dollars and cents with him. It was a bargain and she did not know how to be hard. She felt that she should be on her guard, but she had no shield. She would have signed anything he suggested just to get it over with — just to get out of the office.

But her precipitation in dashing to New York, which had worked out badly in regard to Helen, saved her here. Mr. Britton had not expected her to come so soon. He had been away for the week-end and so had not had time to prepare a contract. He brought the interview to an end by asking her to come the next day to sign up.

Eunice was trembling all over when she got back to the hotel. It was time for lunch, but she had no thought of that. She could scarcely find strength to take off her hat and coat before tumbling on the bed. Tired as her body was, in spite of the bursting pain in her head, the hurt to her soul was worse. She was filled with a new and distressing resentment. She had never had to distrust any one before. She knew that Mr. Britton was trying in some way to take advantage of her and — this was the worst of it — she would have to see him again on the morrow. Why — why had she ever come to this cruel city?

Just as she reached the very bottom of the slough of despond, Helen burst in on her. The letter, forwarded to Albany, had reached her at breakfast and, dropping her work, she had hurried down to New York on the first train to be of help. One glance at the disconsolate heap on the bed which was Eunice made her very glad that she had come — Eunice so obviously needed help. In West Newleigh the neighbors would have called Helen " capable," in New York her friends said that she was " efficient." It did not take her five minutes to get the situation in hand. What had really troubled Eunice most had been the worry, and now, with Helen at her side, there was no more any reason to worry.

First of all Helen straightened her out on the bed and arranged the pillows where they would do the most good. Then she sent for some chicken broth and telephoned to the Maternity Hospital for Mary Dutton.

"Now," she said, sitting down in the old, accustomed attitude on the foot of the bed, "tell me all about it."

The broth was a great source of comfort and gave Eunice strength to tell her story.

"I'll put Win on that job," Helen said, when Eunice had told of her interview with Mr. Britton. "He's had a lot of books published and knows all about contracts."

Thus another worry was lifted from Eunice's shoulders — she would not have to face Mr. Britton again alone — and presently Mary came in with a white-haired old gentleman.

"Hello!" she said cheerily. "I don't have to be introduced, Helen has told me so much about you. This is Dr. Riggs. He was just through at the hospital and I brought him along on the off chance that he might be of use."

"Oh, I don't need a doctor," Eunice protested. "I'm only tired."

"If you don't mind," he said, "I'll look you over. People who are really well don't get tired easily."

She thought that she would have to tell him about her ailments — something she always hated to do — but he stopped her little speech by sticking a thermometer in her mouth. His hands were very large and looked awkward, but they were sure and strangely soothing. Rolling back the lids, he looked deeply into her eyes. Putting down his ear, he listened a long time to the sob and sough of her tired heart. All the while he did not ask a question.

Helen and Mary stood at the foot of the bed watching the proceedings, and it seemed to Eunice that they had their arms about her.

"Stay in bed this afternoon," he said, getting up abruptly, "go out and sit in the Square in the morning, if it's funny. See your friends. Have a good time. Don't mope. But take things easy, you mustn't get tired like this." He consulted his engagement book. "Come to my office Wednesday morning — ten-thirty. I'll give you a thorough examination. I'll leave a prescription at the drug store and have it sent up at once. Good-by."

"I've nothing to do this afternoon but write some letters," Mary said to Helen, when the doctor had left. "I might just as well do it here. So, if you're busy, run along."

"Oh, I hate to be such a bother," Eunice said.

But they just laughed at her. Helen said that she was busy and, promising to be back at five, hurried off to her office.

Mary bet Eunice that she could get her into her nightgown and under the sheets without raising her head three inches.

"Oh, of course you could do it yourself, but I like to show off. Watch me."—"Helen told us that you have beautiful hair," she said as she exhibited her skill, "but I did not expect it to be so marvelous."

"You're not at all what I expected, either," Eunice said; "Helen told me so much about your work — saving the babies. I expected to be very much in awe of you — a little afraid. But I'm not. I don't believe anybody could be afraid of you."

"Oh, yes, they could be. I know one person anyhow who is — the man I'm threatening to marry. He's scared stiff."

"I don't believe it."

But the argument was interrupted by the arrival of the medicine which Dr. Riggs had ordered.

"It was a laugh on me," Mary said as she brought the powder and a glass of water. "There wasn't any reason for me to drag Dr. Riggs over here. I could have prescribed this powder myself — it's just to put you to sleep."

"Oh, there's no use pretending. I know what's the matter with me. But I've been so much better of late that I didn't think I'd get tired so easily. But you started to tell me about the man you are going to marry. I don't believe he's afraid of you."

"Yes, he is. He eats out of the hand. But if I begin talking about Freddie, you'll never get to sleep — and besides I want to write to him."

Eunice lay there very comfortably, watching Mary bent over the paper. Whatever Helen's other talents, she was not good at describing people. Eunice had expected Mary to be so different, rather austere — and thin. She was all soft curves and graciousness and merry smiles.

The sight of her, writing to the man she loved, stirred all sorts of drowsy speculations. How would it feel to be in love? What sort of a man would Mary care for? Of one thing Eunice was sure — he was a lucky dog!

How the city had changed for her in these few hours! All the morning it had seemed soulless and hostile. But Mary and this famous doctor were more lovable than the people she had known in West Newleigh. And Helen was so wonderful.

Gradually every sound — even the noisy traffic of the street — became faint. She heard the blast of a steamship's siren — it sounded so very far away — — perhaps halfway to Europe. The scratching of Mary's pen took on the sound of a loving human voice, singing a low and opiate lullaby.

When Eunice woke up, the morning sun was shining in through the windows. Helen, already arrayed for her day's work, was smiling at her cheerily. It took her several dazed moments to realize that she had slept all through the afternoon and the night as well.

The next few weeks passed for Eunice like what the magazine trade calls "a sunshine serial." It seemed altogether too good to be true. Everybody did things for her, as though to make her forget that first unfriendly morning. Certainly, Helen never realized how valuable she was to Eunice in this crisis.

With royal generosity, Helen shared her friends. Win's business advice was only the most obvious move in the conspiracy of helpfulness. The contracts he arranged for Eunice were very much better than she could have hoped to obtain by herself. And he was very insistent that, if she wanted a good job on her book, she ought to stay in the city to see it through the press. Helen jumped at the idea. She was a bit tired of life in the Settlement. She was really too busy to give much time to the work there and there were many applicants for her place. She found a vacant apartment near the Square which just fitted them. Even after the popularity of her work had grown and her income had increased greatly, Eunice could never have arranged her life so comfortably as Helen did it for her. Helen loved to manage things, she loved details — she even liked to keep accounts. So Eunice did not have to waste any of her scant energy on such harassing details. The "Flat," as they called the new establishment, soon won a place for itself beside the "Studio" and "The Diggings" as an accepted rendezvous of the group.

Frank was usually slow at making friendships, but he at once fell captive to Eunice's charm; he helped her greatly in her work and, having a wide acquaintance among the artist folk of the city, he brought

around many of the best illustrators, who shared with
her their knowledge of the technique of the trade.
Irene in her kindergarten could always find plenty
of models. And Mary adopted her. "You're to be
my heir and legatee," she said. "I must prepare your
shoulders to bear my mantle when I go." At every
turn, Eunice found some one of Helen's friends
smoothing out the rough places before her feet.

But of greater value than any of these comforts
and conveniences was the medical aid of Dr. Riggs.
His name was known the world around for his scientific attainments, but only those who had been privi-
leged to come close to him personally realized his
human bigness, the extent to which he exceeded and
transcended the limits of his professions. Helen had
first met him through the Child Labor Committee.
The prestige of his great name had done more than
any other contribution, more than the most generous
check, for the Cause of the Little Children. And
Helen had interested him in the Maternity Hospital.
He loved these ardent young people, who shared with
him the dream of a healthier race to come. Sometimes when he was utterly tired with the tremendous
rush of his work, he would escape to the Settlement
for an evening's rest with them.

His examination of Eunice was so thorough, so
adroit, so understanding that it inspired her with a
happy confidence.

"It's this way," he said, when it was over, "you
have only a little energy. If you want to live a long
time, you must be saving with it. You must not get
tired and worried as you were the first day. You

used up perhaps a year's energy that time. Take things easy. Keep cheerful. There's no use taking medicine. A quiet, happy life is the best we can do for you. And remember that bed is no place to be except at night. Get up every day you possibly can and get outdoors — a walk in the Square at least."

This seemed sensible to Eunice and much more pleasant than taking the endless concoctions, Helen's father, the village doctor, had given her.

"There's only one medicine I prescribe," he went on, "and the less you take of it the better. It will make you sleep. It's better than insomnia — than tossing about. But that's all I can say for it. Days when you get your lungs full of fresh air, you'll sleep naturally — and that's better than any medicine."

Things went so smoothly and pleasantly for Eunice, thanks to Helen's watchful care, that she had no need to take this medicine for several months. Then Win bought a box at the opera to celebrate the appearance of a new novel.

Eunice had never been to the theater and this night it was "Tristan and Isolde." Such beauty of sight and sound she had never dreamed of, and over and above all the wonders that happened on the stage was the infectious thrill of the great audience, stirred in unison by the magic of the orchestra. "I had never heard any music," Eunice said as she tried to thank Win, "but an ill-tuned piano and phonographs."

As they rode home in the cab, Helen, who sat beside her, felt her trembling spasmodically.

"Tired?" she asked.

"Aren't you?" Eunice was amazed that any one, after such an evening, could be calm. "You're never tired," she added enviously. "You're wonderful!"

That night Eunice could not sleep. Again and again the trembling fit seized her. At last she got up and looked about for the sleeping draught. Helen heard her and called.

"Oh, it's nothing. I'm looking for some medicine to make me sleep."

Helen had inherited from her father an exaggerated, morbid dread of "drugs." She popped out of bed and cross-examined Eunice sharply. It was hard for her to believe that Dr. Riggs had advised "taking drugs." So she went to the hospital the next morning to see him before his clinic.

"It's about Eunice," she said. "Do you approve of her taking drugs to make her sleep?"

He asked a few questions about the cause of her sleeplessness.

"The drug will put her to sleep — spare her a little pain and discomfort. Even drugs will do her no harm — it takes too long a time for them to form a habit."

"Is it as bad at that?"

She was breathless with a sudden realization that her friend's condition was so much more serious than she had let herself believe. He nodded gravely.

"Oh, doctor, why didn't you tell me? I'm afraid I've been unkind."

"You've been kinder than you could have been if I had told you. You've been treating her as if she were really alive. That's best for her. I suppose she knows, people in her condition always do — somehow.

But we must never remind her. You have done more for her than I. Your cheerful manner is better than any medicine. It will come — when it comes — speedily and with no pain, I hope. There is little any one can do for her body. You have done — and, now that the habit is formed, will continue to do — a great deal for her peace of mind. Do not let her know our fears. Treat her as if she were a regular person. Keep her gay and active. Boss her about, don't let her mope. Only don't let her get over-tired. Above all be as merry as you can be yourself."

"Isn't there any hope?"

Dr. Riggs twisted his watch chain for a moment and then looked up at her with a weary but wonderful, marvelous smile.

"Such things are sheer mystery to me; the only explanation is the Christian belief. We would understand," he went on in reply to Helen's blank look, "that God was jealous of us — wanted for Himself the joy of her company."

There were many waiting for the doctor in the clinic. There was nothing more to be said and Helen started to go.

"It is not an easy rôle for you, Miss Cash," he said, putting a hand on her shoulder. "But it is not an easy rôle for me, either. We doctors have to get used to losing our patients. Death always defeats us in the end. We cannot be as impersonal about our cases as we are supposed to be. Something in your friend's sweet courage has taken hold of my imagination. My own daughter died — very long ago. I think that, if she had lived, she might have been like your friend.

There is almost nothing I can do for her, so I count on you."

"But I'm so ignorant about such——"

"You have already done wonders. Really, very much more than I. Together"— the grip on her shoulder tightened —"we will cheat God of her company as long as we can."

It was not an easy rôle for Helen. Before this talk she had not realized that Eunice was as sick as, most unfortunately, she was. Health never can understand and sympathize with illness, and Helen had always believed that the less one thought about bodily weakness the better. She was naturally cheerful, but she had gone out of her way to laugh at her own physical discomforts for Eunice's benefit. Her instinctive brusqueness in such matters she had emphasized in this case.

Now her spirit wanted to speak softly before Eunice, to walk on tiptoe. But her mind obeyed the doctor and stamped about and slammed the doors and laughed uproariously. Intentionally she increased her affected callousness. She often wondered if Eunice saw through the pose. And sometimes Eunice wondered if this manner sprang from gross uncomprehension or from marvelous solicitude. It often jarred on her and sometimes vexed her beyond words, but on the whole she was glad of it. She did not want pity.

Probably nothing which Helen did for Eunice helped her so much as this carefully studied appearance of lack of sympathy. In her aunt's home, sickness had been an ever-present reality which no one

could even momentarily forget. Helen breezily
ignored its existence. In this new life, Eunice found
people thinking and talking of other things, and
sometimes for hours on end she forgot that she was
ill. There was nothing in the atmosphere which
–Helen created to remind her of it. Like most invalids
she was inclined to be supersensitive and timid, but
she could never be frightened, with Helen's calm and
sturdy assurance to support her.

Inevitably a large part of Eunice's life was secondhand. Almost all she knew of the city, this bewilder-
ing new world, she learned through Helen or Helen's
friends. It was a fortunate month if she got out of
doors every day. The fatigues of riding up the
Avenue in a bus to look at the pictures in the Metropolitan had to be paid for by an afternoon in bed.
To go out at night to a theater or a concert was a
great event. So she saw the world very largely
through Helen's eyes — as through colored glasses.

To be sure there was a treasure house in the inmost
citadel of her spirit where she stored away her own
impressions of life. Pondering things over in the
leisure of her frequent solitudes — when her friend
was out in the midst of the traffic — she reached truer
and more subtle judgments. But it was very rarely
that she exhibited any of these private treasures to
others. In far and away most of the matters, which
came to her attention, Helen was very much better
informed than she. While she did not always agree
with her friend's dictums, she seldom disputed them.

CHAPTER IV

SUNDAY BREAKFAST

When Frank Lockwood had married Lillian, Win had, of course, had to leave the Studio where they had lived together so long. Luckily Professor Lancaster had found it necessary to move uptown to be nearer the university, so Win had moved into " The Diggings " with Pete McGee. It was to this apartment, overlooking the Square, that he had invited his friends for Sunday breakfast to meet the Stranger.

The large study was wainscoted with bookshelves. There were volumes of law reports, congressional records, enclycopedias of social reforms, and so forth which represented McGee's habit of mind. Scattered through the shelves was a very fair assortment of the world's best literature of Win's selection.

The mantelshelf over the fireplace, where Win was coaxing the coals into a welcoming blaze, was reserved for " the firm's output." At one end were his two volumes of verse, his " History of King Philip's War," and his string of novels. At the other end were a score or more of unbound pamphlets, in each of which Pete argued for or against some bill which had been before the New York State legislature.

Win had spread on his writing table a Russian bridal apron, heavy, hand-woven linen on the borders of which some long-forgotten peasant girl had em-

53

broidered all the dreams of her maidenhood. A copper coffee percolator bubbled and purred over an alcohol lamp. A pile of oranges on a silver plate sat between a dish of hot buns and a great Viennese *"nusskuchen."* There was also an inelegant, squat bottle of cream.

A few minutes after nine there was a thumping at the door and in came the Lockwoods, Helen and Eunice.

Eunice, although she was manifestly frail, was in nowise gaunt. Helen was a finely built woman, strikingly healthy, but if she had fallen ill and lost a little flesh her bones would have shown through. If Eunice had any bones at all they were very small and slender. There was in her great eyes something of a child's trustfulnss and unconscious purity, which kept most men from falling in love with her. Generally her expression seemed detached and far away, but when some interest lit it with a sudden smile, she seemed startlingly close. Her skin was so soft and fine that it hardly seemed to be there. It was almost as though there were no sharply drawn limit between herself and the circumambient air. And the mass of her golden hair, going brown in the shadows, was quite wonderful.

The greetings had the ring of long-established, informal friendship.

"It's too bad," Lillian said, "that Pete isn't here to make us laugh."

"Is your Stranger coming?" Helen asked.

"I told him to come as soon as, he heard what sounded like a riot here."

As he spoke there was a knock at the door. Win went to open it and introduced Mr. Lane.

The Stranger's manner was the opposite from rigid; it was something between slouchiness and grace. He was evidently abashed by the company and as evidently anxious to be agreeable.

Frank, with his artist's eye, saw the easy movements of his well-conditioned muscles beneath his clothes. The women all wondered how old he was. There was a suggestion of boyishness about him, which was heightened by his embarrassment. But his face, an intelligent, meager Scotch face, was mature.

His dress was inconspicuous, except for a very old-fashioned collar. Helen noticed the queer collar. Lillian, seeing that his trousers were properly pressed, decided that he was a gentleman. Eunice caught the eager and constant question in his eyes.

"The coffee isn't quite ready," Win said. "We'd best stave off hunger with smoke. Here are some marvelous cigarettes to which Mr. Lane introduced me."

"Where do you get them?" Frank asked as he lit one. "They *are good*. You'll have to lead me to them."

"A friend makes them. An Armenian. It is amusing. He is a dealer in Oriental curios and also he is a great smoker — a real connoisseur. He could not be happy without the best. He cannot afford to import fine Turkish tobaccos for his own use alone, so he makes and sells enough to pay for his luxury. It does not make him rich, but gives him great contentment. It is the same with coffee. He imports the finest Aden coffee — enough for commerce to pay his own pleasure. One cannot get better Turkish coffee in Stamboul."

"I've always wanted to taste some real Turkish coffee," Helen said.

"I have some every morning. There is some even now in my room. Perhaps — but, no — Mr. Mathews is making coffee for us."

"Let's have some of yours," Win said. "I invite competition."

Lane opened the window overlooking the Square, and called some mysterious words in an unknown tongue. The window of his apartment opened and there was a conversation in strange gutturals. Presently a young man, his head adorned by a red fez, appeared with a brass tray which held three tiny cups of steaming black coffee. Bowing profoundly, he offered them to the ladies.

"I can make some more in two minutes for the gentlemen," he said.

Frank and Win both said they would like to try it, if it were not too much trouble.

"No trouble at all," Lane said. "He'll make some more," and he spoke again in Turkish. The young man in the fez bowed and hurried out.

"What good English your servant speaks," Lillian said when he had disappeared.

"He is not my servant. We share those rooms together."

"You order him about," Lillian said, "like a servant."

"No, he is not a servant. He is employed in the Turkish consulate. But he is younger than I."

"Well," Eunice said, "if he's your friend, why doesn't he join us?"

"Mr. Mathews did not invite him," Lane said, with some confusion.

"I've not met him," Win said. "We'll have him in, by all means."

So when the young man returned with more coffee he was introduced as Ali Zaky Bey. In every way he was more assured than Lane. He started a glib, fashionable conversation with Helen and Lillian, in which he made a parade of his knowledge of New York slang and continually referred to his acquaintances among the rich and powerful, who live uptown.

Frank and Win and Eunice talked to Lane.

As they were finishing their breakfast there was a new commotion at the door and Professor Lancaster came in with a white-haired old gentleman whom he started to introduce as the renowned Russian revolutionist, Dmitri Inslavsky.

The introductions were still in progress when Inslavsky, who seemed half provoked at being brought into so carefree an assembly, caught sight of Lane.

"*Tovarish*," he exploded in Russian.

He grasped Lane by both shoulders, turned him toward the window to make sure his eyes had not deceived him, and kissed him resoundingly on both cheeks.

Having found a friend, it was only grudgingly that the old man remembered to be courteous to the others.

"It is," he said in his halting English, "that I knew him — long ago — in Russia. Oh, yes! And to find the boy here! It is fifteen years. I thought he must be dead. He is so brave. I must go with him — somewhere; a talk — yes, yes, a long talk. There are many things I must ask him — yes — a long talk. To him I owe more than my life — yes — much more. A fine boy!" There were tears in the old man's eyes as he patted Lane's back. "Yes, a fine boy. And skillful with disguises — very skillful. Yes, and brave——" He waved his hands in gesture of the superlative.

Lane was mightily embarrassed at the demonstration of affection, at the eulogy, at being so abruptly thrust into the limelight. He fairly shrank with distress.

"If it is proper — to leave like this," he stammered, "I will take him to my room."

"Of course it's all right," Win assured him. "Old friends come first. We're glad to have helped you find each other."

"Yes," Lane replied, apparently not altogether pleased. "Thank you. But it was very pleasant to meet you all. I do not know many Americans. I hope — perhaps — some other time——"

He glanced around uncertainly, first at the men, then at the women, especially at Eunice, as if she of all those unfamiliar people might understand his embarrassment, his wish to be cordial, his fear of pushing himself where he was not welcomed.

"Sure," Win said. "We all hope to see more of you."

"We will," Eunice said, with her rare and proximate smile.

"If I come to your room to-morrow afternoon," Frank said, "about five, will you take me to see your Armenian friend?"

"I will be glad to."

"I'll come, too," Win said.

Inslavsky was as impatient as a child. He hardly gave Lane time to make these adieux. Before they were out of the door he threw his arm about the younger man's shoulders and broke into a flood of sonorous Russian, which Lane seemed to understand quite as easily as Turkish and English.

As soon as they had left, Ali Zaky Bey got up imperturbably and announced that, to his profound regret, the Ottoman Government did not recognize the Christian Sabbath and that he must hurry away to his desk at the consulate.

Speculation broke loose the moment he had disappeared.

"Who is this man Lane?" Lancaster asked.

"That's just the question," Win answered. "Who is he?"

"He seems like a gentleman," Lillian said.

Lancaster, not liking the word "gentleman," opposed this verdict.

"Inslavsky would not have called him '_Tovarish,_' that means 'comrade,' if he had not been a true revolutionist — well, we'll find out about him in time. Anyhow my morning plans are spoiled. I wanted you to have a talk with the old man, Win. His story is wonderful. I want you to write a magazine article about him. It would help a great deal. Sorry I can't fritter away my time with you idlers, but I'm rushed to death. I must run along."

He hurried away to his multitudinous busynesses.

"Well," Win asked, "will he do?"

"He has my vote," Helen said. "He looks interesting."

"When he takes you to that cigarette store, Frank," Lillian said, "you can ask him to dinner; let's see — Tuesday or Thursday. It don't matter. And I'll invite him for Thanksgiving. And, say, how about his friend — this Ali Something Bey? 'Bey' means 'prince,' don't it? We ought to call him 'Your Highness.' He'd make five men, if he'd come, and we could ask that new nurse, Miss Claridge. Irene's anxious to have us take her in."

"We might have her, anyhow," Eunice said. "We don't need to have couples. But I vote against this prince — if that's what 'Bey' means. Mr. Lane doesn't like him. I felt that I'd made a break, the minute I suggested that he should join us."

"Why, Mr. Lane said they were friends," Lillian insisted.

"No. He said they were living together. He doesn't like him."

"I didn't notice that," Helen said. "But the Bey didn't make a hit with me. He's too slick."

Lillian did not want to lose her prince. But no amount of argument could shake Eunice's conviction that Lane did not like his roommate.

"When a woman cannot produce reasons for an

opinion," Win said, quoting from his last novel, " she's quite likely right."

" That's the cheapest thing you ever wrote," Helen snorted indignantly.

" Yes," Frank agreed. " It's such an unmarried epigram. It sounds so bachelorish."

But Lillian was too intent on her Thangsgiving project to allow herself to be distracted by such by-play. In her mind there should always be a man for every woman. She would not hear of an odd number. So it was decided that the party should consist of the Lockwoods, Helen and Eunice, Lancaster and Irene, Win and this Mr. Lane.

When this was decided the guests departed. And Win, after clearing away his breakfast wreckage, spread out his papers and settled down to work.

Lillian always spent Sundays with her parents. Helen hurried off uptown with her, and Eunice walked across the Square with Frank to the Studio.

CHAPTER V

LOVE AND THE OTHERS

Of all the friends in the city to whom Helen had introduced her, Eunice felt closest to Frank. It sometimes seemed to her as though her illness were a magic cloak of invisibility, which allowed her to wander unnoticed into the lives of her friends, to penetrate more deeply into their intimacies than was permitted to those who were well. The fact was true enough — people did not pull down the blinds at her approach, arrange the drapery of their veils, nor stiffen into a pose. But the explanation she gave herself for this fact was all wrong. Sickness had nothing to do with it.

Her curiosity about life was so eager and naïve, her interest in people so friendly, her sympathetic understanding so sure — so uncensorious — that no one felt it offensive. It was charming. People found it easy — and safe — to be relaxed and off their guard with her. These new friends, as Helen had always been, were unashamed and unreserved before her.

There was something elusive about Frank. Sooner or later his friends found a door that was closed. He was cordial and approachable; no one could say that he kept them at arm's-length. But he kept every one back a finger's breadth from the threshold of his Inner Shrine. In the first years of his marriage he had tried to tempt Lillian across it. But she was not interested. She did not understand his goddess. His efforts to initiate her into the cult had bored her. This rebuff had only made him the more sensitive about it, the more careful to keep the door of the Sanctuary closed. But he had opened it — at first very shyly — to Eunice.

To be sure, she had become more quickly and easily acquainted with Win. Often, when he saw her from his window taking her morning walk in the Square, he would come out and join her. He had told her all about his own life — his struggle to break away from his Bostonian heritage. "The trouble with me," he said, "is that I'm too damned refined — cursed with culture." He told her of the years of his youth he had wasted, trying to revive the brave old traditions of New England letters — his transcendental sonnets, his volume of essays on "Taste," his "History of King Philip's War." "The only thing I can say for myself is that I wasn't flippant. God knows I took myself seriously. I wanted to write, but I wasted my time on the kind of things people expected me to do. I didn't write those sonnets because there was an emotion in me yearning for expression — but because they had written verses at Brook Farm. My essays! I didn't have anything to say, but they told me that the essay was a noble form of literature, shamefully neglected by this commercial age. I spent three years on that history — not because any one was interested in a third-rate scrimmage with the Indians — I wasn't interested myself — but history came after verses and essays."

"I don't believe you were such a fool," Eunice said.

"Yes, I was. But I never had a chance. My parents caught me too young. Prescott, of the Fine Phrases, Emerson, Apostle of the Obvious — those were the only ideals they gave men. That's Boston! Culture! — not as a weapon in a crusade, not as a means to a larger, fuller, more vital life — no, — but culture as an end in itself. And a snobbish end at that! It was Frank who jerked me out of the rut — rescued me from this deadening Bostonism. What the Vandals did to the Roman Empire wasn't a patch on what Frank did to me!

"Once, when we were just getting acquainted, he explained to me why he didn't do the regular stunt of copying the Old Masters in the museum. 'Why should I?' he said; 'I'll never have to paint a Spanish guy in silk tights, nor an altar piece for an Italian church. Why waste time trying to imitate them? If I've any talent at all, I'd better develop it on subjects that interest me.'

"You know," Win went on, "that was a brand-new idea to me — it gave me quite a thrill to speculate about what I might become, if I gave up the idea trying to be like Lowell. Of course at first I thought Frank was a fool. I thought that it was a pity he did not have a background of solid culture. Me — with my little talent for plodding — pitying him! It wasn't till his 'Study in Moonlight Grays' won the Pittsburgh Prize and was bought for the Corcoran, that I began to take him seriously. He fascinated me. He was the first real live person I had ever met. When he moved to New York, I came along."

He told her about their first years in the city, how they had found the Studio, and made friends with the Settlement crowd. He told her about his own work, the novels he had written, and the better ones to come. But most of all he talked about his friend.

At the time Eunice reached New York, Frank was not doing much. Six months before, he had finished his "Opus XLVIII." It had been a tremendous effort, leaving him utterly fatigued.

"It's terrifying," Win said, "this living with a genius. Such ups and downs — dizzying high ups and such abysmal downs! When that picture was finished, he went to pieces, lost interest in everything — got drunk! The critics were wild about it. Baldwin bought it for his private collection. But Frank would put his fingers in his ears, if he heard it mentioned. Utter exhaustion!

"I suppose real creation is always exhausting. A mother, they say, must rest a while from her travail before she can find energy to love the child. Perhaps that's why the great God has let this world of His run so amazingly awry. After the six days of His labor, He was probably too tired to care. When His long Sabbath has rested Him, He may begin to take an interest in what His creatures are doing. Anyhow, that's the way it was with Frank. It was months before he could paint again. Irene got him started at last on that Mother Goose frieze for her Kindergarten."

Such stories about Frank served to whet Eunice's desire to know him better, and at last the chance came when he asked her to pose for a poster he had promised the Drama League.

It was not so easy to get acquainted with him as it had been with Win. He was not a ready talker. Generally he had some brushes in his mouth and, when he did not, he conversed visibly, but inaudibly, with himself. To be sure he looked at her a great deal, but with no appearance of recognition. "He would look in just the same way at a bunch of carrots," she told Helen, "if he were painting a still-life."

But in spite of his conversational failings, Eunice did get acquainted with him. He was not always silent. Sometimes, during the rest period, he talked a little — never about himself, but always about something close to him. His favorite brand of colors; the best place to buy canvases; disconnected scraps about the technique of his art. Some of it was directly useful to her in her own work, and once a question of hers about perspective — a matter which always troubled her — set him off on a very helpful discourse.

Running through all his stray remarks, perhaps even more through his silences, was evidence of a very real devotion. No detail that affected the service of his goddess was beneath his serious attention.

"The artist," he said, "is nothing but a tool. He must grind his edges sharp. That's what people who don't know call 'drudgery.' No real artist ever called it that."—— "A picture is not something an artist does. The goddess does it by means of him."—— "The goddess comes only now and then. You can't tell when she'll come. So you must work hard — keep your edges sharp all the time. It would be awful to be dull if she came and wanted to use you.—— That's why I work hard on this poster, which doesn't matter — to keep my edges sharp."

—— "It's a long time since the goddess has come to me. I don't want to get rusty."

But in all he said and did, his faith that the goddess would come again was implicit.

When the poster was finished, he tried to thank her for posing, but she cut him short. "It's been a favor to me. You see, I've never been to a school. I've never seen any one paint before. I've learned a great deal — just watching you."

"If that's the way you feel," he said, "come in any time. I don't like people about when I work, generally. But you've sense enough not to interrupt. Come in any time."

She took advantage of his offer and a habit was formed, which she valued highly. Two or three times a week, she would drop into his Studio for an hour or more. A very real friendship developed, and so it happened that Eunice was the first of the group to hear of Lillian von Lehrenburg.

She had come into the Studio one morning and found Frank, disheveled, in evening clothes, working furiously at some sketches. But for once he wanted to stop and talk.

"I've found her!" he said with intense excitement. "My next picture! Magnificent! Gorgeous! Not even Leonardo ever had such a model! The goddess found her for me — she's come again. And — thank all the gods — I'm ready."

Eunice had never seen Frank so exalted. This was what Win had meant by his being "way up" and she wondered if it would be followed by an "abysmal down."

"She's not lovely," he said, walking about nervously, "nothing soft like that — beauty — sheer beauty! Teutonic. The marvelous Nordic blonde. I've always dreamed of it., One model has exquisite hands. There's a girl up at The Art Students' League with an almost perfect torso — but her skin coloring is bad. And the last model I had — her face was a joy to paint. So it goes — an ideal made out of patchwork. And now — suddenly — I find it — all embodied — full, queenly beauty — sovereign! And such marvelous symmetry. I never saw anything like the way her arms hang onto her shoulders — the sweep of them!

"Where did I find her? At a dinner party. I hate such stiff formality — I don't go to a dinner once a year. But last night — the goddess sent me — guided my footsteps. And there she was.

"Her parents were there, too, so I could get it all arranged. The mother's a fool — typical 'lady thug' — spattered with paste jewels — at least I think they were paste. She wanted a society portrait effect — hand on a Russian wolfhound and all that. But the old man has some sense. I'm to do just as I please. They're to come this afternoon. I dashed down here to get started. What do you think of these sketches?

"See. And here's a bolt of old brocade — cloth of gold. I saw it once in a shop window and bought it. Win was furious. I was awful hard up those days and he called it extravagance. But I knew it would come in handy. The goddess told me to buy it. It will make a wonderful robe for her. Square cut in the neck. A great braid over this shoulder — it emphasizes the curve of her arm. In one hand a crystal globe — a high light — gold in her gown — gold chair — and the gold of her hair. In the other hand an upright, naked sword — a straight and cruel sword. And a crown — just a band of graven gold. See, here's a design I've made for a chain to hang about her neck — flat, square links. I know a theatrical property man who will make just what I want. A necklace for the bride of Charlemagne.

"Oh! Do you see it? Her head bent just a trifle forward — gazing down into the crystal. It's *the* Picture!"

Eunice, never having encountered such excitement before, hardly knew what to say, but a practical suggestion, worthy of Helen, occurred to her.

"You haven't been in bed all night. You'll have to change your clothes. You'd best get a little sleep."

"Sleep!" he said scornfully, as though it were an utter impossibility. "But I guess I had best wash up a bit and get something to eat. Come to think about it, I'm famished. Oh! my friend," he said, twirling around on his heel in glee, "it's good to be at work again! — Don't tell anybody about it," he added as she turned to go. "I can't talk about it till I get well started. I haven't even told Win. I guess he thinks

I came home drunk. I wouldn't talk to him at all this morning.

Eunice asked if she could come in to watch him as usual.

"Wait a couple of weeks," he said, "till I get well into it."

Ten days or so later, Win came out of the Studio one morning and joined Eunice in the Square.

"Frank's at work again," he said. "It's just as it was when he was painting his Opus XLVIII. I have to feed him by hand — literally. If I did not stand right over him, he'd forget to eat what I bring. It's awful — awe-inspiring."

"He told me he had found a model. But "— she was surprised at Win's disconsolate tone —" aren't you glad he's at work again?"

"Oh, yes, of course; but I'm frightened. I'm only too glad to stand by and pour the coffee into him, bring him his lunch and all that. But I've been through it with him before. I haven't any fear for his work — it will be something marvelous — I'm sure of that. But I'm afraid for him. He's putting so much of himself into the job — there'll be precious little of him left."

"Have you seen the girl?"

"Just a glimpse. She doesn't matter — she's only what he calls a tool. But I really am worried about him. Nobody could stand such intensity, day after day, without any let-up. I wish you'd take a hand. I haven't any tact — it always rubs him the wrong way, if I butt in. But he likes you. Why have you stopped coming to the Studio? God knows I don't

want to interfere with his work, but I'm sure he
could work better if now and then he thought of something else. Can't you come to lunch to-day? Fake
up some problem about your work — anything. It
can't do any harm — at worst he'll be rude. It might
do some good."

Eunice considered this proposal a few minutes.
Frank had said that she could come after he got well
started. It would interest her immensely to see him
at work on a great effort. Perhaps Win was right —
it might do some good. And besides she had her
woman's curiosity. She very much wanted to see this
person who had stirred Frank so profoundly.

So at noon she appeared at the Studio with one of
her " Tit, Tat, Toe, and Little Tot " drawings under
her arm. Once more it was " perspective " which
bothered her. Frank saw the trouble at a glance and
righted it. While they were discussing this, lunch
was announced. Frank was not at all rude, the meal
went off very pleasantly.

" Would you like to see how it's coming on? " Frank
asked, when the coffee was finished. Win, joyfully,
escaped upstairs to his writing room. His little conspiracy was working well.

" Somehow," Frank said as he led her into the
Studio, " I can talk to you. It helps. I get tired
of talking to myself."

He had already made considerable progress. It
was only scaffolding, but Eunice was enough of an
artist herself to catch an intimation of what it was
to be. He was keeping close to the design he had
first shown her. There was no stumbling. " The

Picture" had come to him, whole, complete. He
knew just what he wanted to do. He argued it all
out with her. It was more of a lecture than a conversation. He was not asking any one's advice.

A few minutes before two, Mother von Lehrenburg
and her daughter arrived. Eunice looked right past
the mother. There was nothing about her to hold any
one's attention. The daughter, as Frank had said,
was quite wonderful. Larger than the average, she
was nevertheless lithe and graceful. Her hair was
almost as heavy as Eunice's, a shade or two lighter
in color. The features of her face as well as her
form were as nearly perfect as Eunice had ever seen.
But there was one slight reservation in her admiration. There was something lacking in her eyes. It
was not that they were ugly — just somewhat less
beautiful than the rest. They made Eunice think
instinctively of the blank eyes of a statue. "That's
why he paints her looking down at the crystal," she
said to herself, with sudden appreciation of his in-
sight. "They won't show in his picture. It will be
all beautiful."

The introductions were awkward, for Frank was not
adroit in such matters. Lillian went to the dressing
room to change into costume and Frank began laying
out his brushes, so Eunice had to talk to the mother.
Mrs. von Lehrenburg stared at her hostilely through
her lorgnette. Her voice was harsh and nagging.
Used to people who did not consider her very highly,
she had become unpleasantly self-assertive. Eunice
saw that Frank's estimate had been right, the jewels
were paste. "She must have been beautiful, too,

once — *sic transit tyrannis.*" Eunice was fond of quotations, but a trifle weak in Latin.

When Lillian appeared in her crown and cloth of gold, Eunice's heart almost stopped beating. " Why wasn't she born centuries ago, when she might have been the queen of some great conqueror? " Seated in the high-backed Gothic chair, which Frank had gilded, the effect was regal indeed.

Frank stood and gazed at her a moment after she had taken her pose, then he beckoned to Eunice.

"Look," he said. " Look at the shadows on her throat — and the texture of the skin on her cheek."

A deep, angry blush broke over Lillian's face; it spread down to her throat. She hung her head.

"Oh!" Frank groaned in vexation, "you moved. The pose was perfect. Can you get it again? Please. The chin a little higher."

Eunice, although she blushed in sympathy with Lillian, was amused. Frank was utterly unconscious that the very objectivity of his admiration was almost insulting. "She might just as well be a bunch of carrots," she thought, remembering her own experience.

Eunice felt herself *de trop;* her presence rendered Lillian uncomfortable and self-conscious. So at the first rest period, she slipped away. " I'll not embarrass them again," she said to herself.

Back in her own room, Eunice thought over the experience in great detail, as was her wont. She was most impressed by the obvious difference in the way that Frank and she looked at this beautiful person. He saw beauty; she saw a person. She doubted if Frank had the least curiosity about Lillian's life and thoughts and ideals. To him she was a model, an amazing, thrilling thing to paint. But Eunice was immensely curious. She wondered how it would feel to know oneself so beautiful — for Lillian surely knew. She wondered from what soil, from what seed this marvelous thing had sprung.

Eunice, after this first encounter with Lillian, did not go again to the Studio. Once or twice, carrying out Win's suggestion, she asked Frank to come to lunch at the Flat to help her with her work. So she was kept somewhat in touch with his progress, and was not surprised when he called up on the telephone and said it was finished.

" I'm inviting all the crowd," he said, " for a private view — to-morrow afternoon — for tea —four-thirty."

Helen was a little delayed at her office that day, so the rest of the friends were already at the Studio when the two girls arrived.

Eunice, although she had followed its earlier stages, was completely surprised and overwhelmed by the Picture. It so much exceeded her expectations that she was reduced to an awed speechlessness. She sat down on a divan a little apart from the groups about the tea table. She heard only vague scraps of the conversation. De Pargt, the curator of the museum, and Baldwin, who had bought the Opus XLVIII, had been there earlier in the afternoon and Baldwin had bought it for the Metropolitan. This much Eunice heard of the talk, but she was too intent on the Picture to listen. She had a vivid feeling that now at last she was really acquainted with Frank.

Presently Helen came over and sat beside her.
"What do you think of it?" Eunice waved her
hands vaguely. Pantomime was a trick she had
learned from the children. She could express very
much more by gestures than most civilized adults.

"Of course, it's wonderfully good," Helen said,
"but do you think he meant to give it that hard —
almost merciless — tone?"

"Yes, I think that is just what he meant. He told
me before he began that it would be beautiful — not
lovely. There's a big difference."

Helen started to say something more, but there was
a tumultuous ring at the door. Frank went to answer
it. A loud, rather coarse, voice greeted him.

"I ran across De Pargt just now and he said you
had something wonderful down here. Can I see it?"

"Bruce Lyons," Helen said disgustedly.

All of them knew Lyons, none of them liked him.
He was a man shading toward fifty. He wrote popular novel serials in a magazine of a million odd
subscribers. He put what he called "twang" into
his stories, not the frank, joyous obscenity of Rabelais,
but an indecently veiled salaciousness. He had the
gift of words, of full-sounding, sonorous words. His
advertising methods were blatant and successful. He
lived uptown expensively, with an expensive wife.

But this prosperous dealer in cheap vulgarities had
once been young. Years ago, he had lived in a garret
in Paris, trying to write the Great American Play.
But of those years he never spoke and so Frank and
Win could not understand why he sometimes came to
the Studio and always outstayed his welcome. But

the explanation was simple; he immensely admired these two young men who had kept the faith, At times, when the din of his facile typewriter became unbearable, he would jump into his gaudy limousine and come down to the Studio to listen to their talk of the goddess, whose cult he had served in his youth — to worship, vicariously and from afar, at the shrine he had deserted.

The Picture stood on an easel directly opposite the door, so the unwelcomed guest saw it before catching sight of the tea party.

"Lord God Almighty!" he exclaimed. "It isn't fair. You ought to warn a man. I've come in with my hat on."

Snatching off his hat, he stood there a moment uncovered before the Picture.

"That's her!" he said reverently. "The goddess! She's been here, Frank, and has smiled on you. Good Lord! How I envy you!"

Then, turning from it reluctantly, he shook hands with the guests. He was noticeably subdued. As soon as he decently could, he returned to the Picture.

Suddenly he began blinking his eyes, but the tears, the foolish tears, could not be hid.

"You people despise me — and ought to! I didn't like to be hungry. The mess of pottage smelt good. I never saw the goddess — face to face — as you have, Frank. I didn't deserve to. But now and then — I caught some of the effulgence of her nearness — but — well — I wasn't man enough! I haven't any right even to look at your picture of her!"

Without a word of farewell, he grabbed his hat and rushed out.

"Well," Helen said, "he's the last man I ever expected to see get hysterical."

But to Eunice, sitting silent on the divan, this strange outburst seemed a poignant soul tragedy. Another thwarted life! It was only a variation of her own tragedy. In the old days in West Newleigh, she had longed for life in the vaguest terms. She had hungered for — she knew not what. She had had no clear picture of what life might mean to her if she were well. But since she had come to New York, since her talks with Win about literature, since her slow-growing friendship for Frank had ripened, life had come to mean for her something quite precise. The thing she hungered for was also the goal of their aspirations, The Holy Grail of their questing. If she had only been strong enough to stand the long hours before the easel, she, too, might have done brave things! "The Unknown Goddess." That was what she would always call this picture of Frank's. He had shown it to her — what life might be. She, too, would have worshiped at his shrine, if her weak body had not betrayed her. Even so this man, Lyons, had been betrayed by a weakness of the will. She was thankful for the failing light. In their eagerness to discuss the good news of Frank's sale, the others did not notice her tears.

About ten days after this private view, Win telephoned one evening to find if the girls were home. And a few minutes later he appeared, looking utterly disconsolate.

"Frank's going to marry her," he announced.

"The model?" they both asked at once.

He nodded gloomily and then a wry smile came over his face.

"I'm in bad. After I met her the first time, when he'd been working only a few days — I asked him how it was possible for such a beautiful person to be such a pinhead?".

Helen laughed, but Eunice said:

"She is stupid."

"That's the tragedy," Win agreed. "She's awful. This is worse than I feared, worse than getting drunk."

"You don't either of you know her well enough to talk like that," Helen said sensibly. "Frank is the only one who's seen much of her. He's marrying her — not you people. It's his affair."

"It is?" Win said combatively. "I'm not so sure. I'm blue about it, because I'm thinking of his work. That doesn't belong just to him. It belongs to all of us — to all the world. And marrying her won't help it. Why! He says he's going to stop painting and get a regular job as an illustrator — to support her! He's already starting on some drawings for Bruce Lyons' next thriller. It's tragic!"

All the evening they talked it over. Win told and retold all he knew and it was not much. He had been completely surprised by the news. There was nothing for him to do but accept the situation. Luckily, Lancaster was moving uptown, so Win piled his belongings on a cart and moved across the Square to share "The Diggings" with Pete McGee.

The affair seemed just as tragic to Eunice as it did to Win. She could not understand it. She did not take Frank's renunciation of painting very seriously — that was just weariness after the tense burst of work. But somehow, vaguely, she felt that Frank would never paint so well again. Something incalculable and irrational had laid hold of her friend and had twisted him out of his path, out of the road of his destiny. She was grieved, because she felt that in some indefinite way her friend had been lessened.

The marriage also disturbed the other friends. Lillian, the newcomer, was not welcomed. She did her best to be friendly, but she suffered from numerous handicaps. She was too ill-educated to talk intelligently on any subject that interested them. There was a fatuous self-assertiveness about her ignorance which made her simplest conversational efforts a failure. And she seemed to think that as a married woman she could speak with authority to the other girls. Worst of all, she was an idler. She was not even apologetic about it. She seemed to think that being adored was a sufficient occupation.

She would not have been tolerated by any of the friends, if they had not all been so fond of Frank. But he made it very clearly a case of "Love me, love my dog." They could not give him up, so they did their best to be at least formally cordial to her. What he thought about the situation, nobody knew. He gave no sign of any discontent.

As the months passed by, it became evident that,

far from helping Frank in his career, she was allow-
ing him to go, artistically speaking, to the dogs. His
illustrations of Bruce Lyons' novel were a marked
success and one of the best publishing houses in New
York was planning an extensive reprint of the English
classics, in uniform and expensive bindings. The
series was to be a *chef d'œuvre* of the bookmaking art;
they decided that Frank was just the man they needed
for the illustrations and signed him on for a five-year
contract at five thousand a year.

The news of this contract came as a thunderbolt
to the friends. The hostility to Lillian became pas-
sionate. This seemed a definite giving up of his
mission in life. How could she have permitted it?
Often behind his back they discussed whether he was
happy. How could he be with such a woman —
coarse-grained, petty, lacking in all ideals? Win,
who saw most of him, was the most pessimistic. But
their councils came to nothing except a general agree-
ment that, if anybody could do anything, it was
Eunice. They all realized that she had a surer touch
with Frank than the rest of them.

"Why, there's nothing I could do," she would reply
to their vague urgings, but she continually turned
the matter over in her mind. She was reluctant to
interfere, but more than any of them she felt the
tragedy of Frank's renunciation. Herself a mere
illustrator, who mourned that she could not paint,
she felt poignantly the meaning of his sacrifice. And
so, at last, without telling any one that she had decided to act, she telephoned to Frank and asked him
to come around and help her out of a tangle in her

drawing. But her easel was folded up against the wall, when he came.

"I lied to you," she said. "It isn't my drawing at all — that doesn't matter. I wanted to talk with you. Oh, it's impertinent — very personal — none of my business."

She noticed him go tense in a defensive, almost hostile attitude.

"Sit down a minute, please. It's this way, Frank. Doesn't affection give any rights? You must know how we all love you. Remember that line from 'Timon of Athens'—'I am wealthy in my friends'? You're very rich. The first day I was here in New York, I was sick and Mary was taking care of me, telling me about the friends I would meet. 'Frank,' she said, 'you're sure to like him. Everybody does.' And so I've found it. You know we're fond of you. Win especially. He'd go through fire for you.

"And we can't care for you like this without being interested — in your work — in everything that happens to you. It isn't just gossipy curiosity. It's because we love you. And now we're worried — about this illustrating. We'd all set our hearts on your going on with your painting — on and up. Don't you see, Frank, I'm not talking this way just on my own account? — but it's all of us — your friends. Can't you tell us about it — so we'll understand?"

Frank got up and came over to the couch where she lay, took up her hand, and kissed it. Then he walked over to the window, etching designs in the frost, for several minutes. When at last he turned there were tears in his eyes. He drew up a hassock beside the couch and took her hand.

"I don't deserve such friends." He shook his head sharply, as though to drive the huskiness from his voice. "But don't you understand? This is a thing you can't talk about. One doesn't discuss one's wife, even with the best of friends. I'm sure you know — you and the friends — that this is a matter between Lillian and me. I can't talk about it. But it's going to come out all right. That's what I want you to say when you tell them about this talk."

"They don't know we're having it. I won't tell them anything."

"No," he said thoughtfully, "I'd rather you did tell them. I don't want them to think I am snippy or unfriendly. Falling in love with Lillian hasn't had that effect. And you know "— he went on with quiet, sure emphasis —"I *am* in love with her. More now than the day I married her — or the day before. But it hasn't made me value my friends any the less. Only — well — you must all see it, so there's no harm saying it — I have a problem on my hands. A problem I must work out for myself. Lillian is different from you, from all my friends, different from anybody I ever knew. But I don't think you people are quite fair to her. She's never had a decent chance, she hasn't had the opportunities you people have had. Her mother seems to have been the big influence in her life. She's been taught standards of value that are different — wrong, all wrong. 'The Transvaluation of all Values' — that's my job, as I see it. I don't suppose it will be easy, but I'll succeed. So much depends on success — everything for me!"

"As I said," he went on after a long pause, "it's my job — something I can't let out to any subcontractor — however friendly. Marriages aren't made in heaven, they're made in the home. And these intimate things of the home — well — one doesn't talk about them. I know you people's friendliness. It's wonderful — undeserved — infinitely precious. But there's nothing you can do to help me in this job. Nothing but to trust me — to go on being friendly — to me and to her. Yes, that would help. The more she feels that you people are friendly, the easier it will be for me. She wants to learn our ways. And I want her to like you all.

"That's what I wish you'd tell the friends only," — he kissed her hand again —"I know you will say it so much better than I could. I've been afraid to say anything — afraid it might sound as if I were complaining. I'm not — not at all! Don't let them think that for a minute. I couldn't talk to Win — or the others, but — well — thanks to you."

He got up and went again to the window. "This had to be said," he remarked over his shoulder, "but I couldn't say it without help. Thanks."

In a moment he came back to the hassock.

"You and I are both wealthy in our friends. We all love you, too. I do. You are the newest — and best — of my friends and so I can talk to you a little more freely than to the others. You mustn't worry about the illustrating. A few years — what do they matter? And loving — it's really better than painting. Only it's more like sculpture — modeling — flesh and blood — and spirit — instead of cold clay. Think of me that way — working just as hard as you ever saw me work on a picture — harder. But the same old job — trying to make something beautiful — something for the goddess.

"Of course, I hate the illustrating. But it's just as in the early days — when I had to do chores to earn money for my paints. I was a waiter ·in a restaurant once. I loathed it, but that didn't matter — I earned enough to paint my first real picture — 'The Study in Moonlight Grays.' So now I have to do this chore — to finance the bigger job."

"But couldn't you earn quite as much painting? That would keep your edges sharp. They'll get dull at this — dull and rusty."

"Yes," Frank admitted, "there's danger of that. But all the good work I ever did, I did for love. I can't spoil the devotions now by passing the collection basket. ·I couldn't take a fee from the goddess any more than I could charge a price for loving Lillian. It's different when somebody likes what you have done — done for love of doing it, done because you couldn't help doing it — and pays you for it, from sitting down to paint to order. No, I can't paint for money. Least of all now.

"Don't you understand? That's what Lillian and her mother want me to do. That's the standard of value she's learned from her mother — money. I'm trying to make her understand that one doesn't worship for pay. That's my job — to make her understand."

Frank got up abruptly and started to go — as though he had said more than he had intended. But at the doorway, he turned back and came again to her couch.

"Of course, I can't find words to thank you — you and the friends — for your interest. I know it's kind. But I — Oh, I can't say it! All I can do is to kiss your hand once more."

"I don't think Lillian would object," Eunice said, "if you kissed my cheek."

It was in 1908 that Eunice had come to the city. Within a year, Frank had married Lillian, a few months later, Mary's doctor came home from Vienna and carried her off to Calfornia. On all sides, Eunice saw the handiwork of the most capricious of the gods. Herself too ill to dream of love as a personal adventure, she listened all the more eagerly to the stories others told her.

There was a young girl from the South — on the outer edge of their circle — who had come to New York to paint and had been distracted by a writer of verse, at once "libre" and libertine. Frank and Helen between them had snatched the arsenic bottle from her lips, lent her some money, and found her a job. She sobbed out all the details of this amorous misadventure to Eunice. Insisting that she had always despised the man as much as she had loved him, she lived in constant terror that she might encounter him again by accident and that he might beckon to her.

Then in contrast to this mad lark of Cupid's, Lancaster and Irene — just when the excitement caused

by Frank's wedding was cooling down — announced
their marriage. There had been no foolish whoop-de-
doo about this affair — they had had the knot tied
by a magistrate. They were rather boastful of the
placid and quiet way it which it had been done. They
did not like fireworks. Nothing was changed in their
outward circumstances, Irene kept her maiden name,
went on with her work, continued to live in the Settlement. In fact the only visible effect of the new
arrangement was that it became impossible to find
either of them free for week-end picnics. But behind
this façade of casualness, in which they took an in-
nocent pride, Eunice got glimpses of something vital
and vibrant, some strange, new content to their lives
which she could not wholly comprehend.

For the best part of every day she was alone, walking in the Square, working over her drawings,
stretched out on her couch with a book. In these
solitary hours, she very often thought over the love
affairs of her friends. Love was something to mull
over and ponder deeply. Just because her interest
was so impersonal, it was the more acute. She read
everything she could find on the subject, from Car-
penter's "Love's Coming of Age" to Havelock Ellis.

Whether or not "Love is Best" she could not decide, but one thing seemed certain — Love is Strongest. No other force, which she could observe, seemed
to her so tremendous. Even the stoutest personalities swayed under its pressure. Helen, usually so
firm, so sure of herself, did not seem firm nor sure
in regard to Pete. Eunice thought about these two
very often. Was it a match? All the rest of the

friends thought it was, but she hoped not. For of all of Helen's friends, she liked Pete least. In this — as she would have admitted herself — she was less than fair to him — she knew him least. When he came to the Flat, it was so obviously to see Helen that Eunice had no chance to get acquainted. But she could readily see why Helen preferred him. Lancaster lived in the world of abstract ideas. Frank and Win had the artist's preoccupation with form. But Pete " got things done "— concrete, tangible things. His work — lobbying reform measures through the State legislature at Albany — was something Helen could grasp. Politics seemed more real to her than philosophy or literature or painting. But while Eunice could see that Helen liked Pete best, it was equally clear to her that Helen was very uncertain as to her personal relations with him.

Other things Helen could bend to her will, but this was something she could not control. Love was an unsolved problem for her. In all her comments on the amorous adventures of her friends, she showed her own uncertainty. She, so decisive in other things, was plainly bluffed.

There had been a long and great intimacy between them. During the fight for the Child Labor Law they had worked together constantly. And this fine, frank friendship seemed to satisfy Helen entirely. She was a partisan of the *Status Quo*. But clearly, it did not satisfy Pete. At frequent intervals, it was obvious to Eunice that he was " spoiling things " again.

Helen ordinarily rode on the floodtide of life. Things went well with her, and the success which commonly crowned her efforts was always earned. She threw herself whole-heartedly, untiringly, into every job she undertook, and she stuck to it till it was finished.

She was blessed with a better brain than most people, direct, incisive, quick at grasping essentials. It had been well trained at college and, sitting at the feet of Experience, she was learning all the time. Above all she was not hasty nor rash. She believed in thinking things out in advance. She had learned that it pays better to have on idea a month that works out, than a dozen a day which go wrong.

Her optimism was not of the fatuous — "God's in His heaven, all's right with the world "— kind. She found the world appallingly wrong, but she had a firm faith in the possibility of putting things right. It seemed to her only a matter of will and skill, of persistent, intelligent effort.

"Spot has entire faith in the last act," Pete said jeeringly, at one of their gatherings. "She's not discouraged by the complications of the earlier scenes. The industrious Dramatist always invents a dénouement — an untying. And Spot — although she will deny it — has faith that the Great Dramatist, who sets the scene on this world stage of ours, will pull off a final curtain which will make the universe applaud."

"Rubbish!" Helen had retorted. "I'm not relying on any Great Dramatist to do our job for us. Your comparison is all wrong. Stage people are only puppets — reciting the lines the author has given them. But we're not puppets. We have wills of our

own. I do have faith in the last act — not because
of any Beneficent Dramatist — but because we can im-
pose our wills on the tangle — untie it ourselves."

"I am the master of my fate," Pete chanted, "the
captain of my soul."

"Well, aren't you?" Helen demanded. "I am."

But if Helen were the captain of her soul, it seemed
to Eunice that her hand on the rudder was singularly
wobbly and uncertain, when it came to steering a fixed
course in regard to Pete.

At times Helen came home on a low tide, more or
less in the dumps, certainly at odds with life. And
Eunice knew that Pete had been "spoiling things"
again. For a year or more they had no conversation
on the subject, but at last her curiosity got the upper
hand.

It had been a silent, moody supper. Helen had had
almost nothing to say.

"What's the matter?" Eunice asked. "Has Pete
been proposing again?"

Helen laughed assent.

"Does it show?" she asked.

"I can generally tell."

Helen talked of other things through the rest of
the meal. But, although she had laid out some papers
to work after supper, she abruptly turned away from
them to talk.

"I don't understand it. I don't understand him.
And sometimes I don't understand myself."

After this sweeping announcement of her fallibility,
she lit a cigarette and made herself comfortable on the
foot of Eunice's couch.

"It isn't a thing you can reason out."

This statement also was a very sweeping departure from her ordinary point of view and she hastened to qualify it.

"At least we don't know enough about this business of falling in love to be sure of our reasoning. There aren't any good textbooks. What's the difference between friendship and love? All we know is that there is a difference — a big difference.

"Now, I like Pete — better than any man I know. I know him best. I know him well — all except this love side of him. I don't understand that — so I'm frightened of it.

"I like to be with him. I like his talk — he's really serious behind his fun-making. Above all, he's a wonderful fellow to work with. When he wants to be, he is a perfect friend. But every once in a while he has a brain storm — spoils everything."

"But," Eunice put in, "you ought to know your own mind by this time. Are you going to marry him?"

"No," Helen said it sharply, without any qualification in her tone.

"No, I'm not going to marry him.— I know what you think," she went on. "If my mind is made up not to marry him, I ought to send him packing. That's the storybook solution. But why should I? Of course, I would be an awful cad if I gave him any encouragement, but I don't. I've told him, a hundred times, that I don't care for him that way. I do value his friendship — immensely — but I've never asked him to hang around.

"I don't like the storybook solution. It's too simple — and the problem isn't simple. After all, we're grown-up people. We have our work to do. Shall I resign from The Child Labor Committee, just because he thinks he's in love with me? Shall I ask him to stop working for the law — so I won't have to see him? Shall I ask him to move away from New York and give up all his friends here, because the sight of him offends me? It doesn't, you know. Or shall I cut loose and look for a job in Chicago?

"No, that seems to me foolish. I put it up to him just as straight as I can. And as far as getting married goes — there's nothing doing! I say to him — let's accept that fact — forget it — go on with our work together, our solid, fine, old friendship."

"What does he say?" Eunice asked.

"It doesn't matter what he says," Helen replied wearily. "One time he says this — the next time he says that. Sometimes he's fine about it — shakes hands in good-fellowship and all goes well — for a while. Sometimes he storms and rages — storms out of the room and goes off to Albany for a week or so. But pretty soon he comes to his senses — full of apologies and good intentions — and things go smoothly again for a while. But it doesn't matter what he says. Pretty soon he gets moody and dejected — oh, I can see it coming. I do the best I can to prevent it, but he breaks out again. And it takes it out of me. To-day it was fierce."

Eunice kept breathlessly still, in breathless curiosity.

"My cigarette's gone out," Helen said, getting up

for a match. She walked nervously, puffing to get the light well started. "It was disgusting!" She stopped in front of Eunice. "It makes me mad — to get stirred up like this. It's so senseless. He came into the office just before closing time and as soon as the girls had gone he broke loose. Worse than usual — a lot! I suppose some one had been telling him —'Faint heart ne'er won fair lady, ho' or such rot. Perhaps he'd been reading a Jack London caveman story. Anyhow that's the way he acted — tried to carry things by storm! · It was so idiotic!

"This time I'm really angry. I suppose I'll just have to make up my mind to it — that a woman can't have decent friendships with men. It's *tout ou rien* with them. Just because I don't want to sit in his lap and be pawed over, I must give up this old friendship. It makes me sick!"

"But don't you want to get married?" Eunice asked. "Ever?"

"That's the funny part of it," Helen said, sitting down. "Of course I do. When I was a girl I didn't like children. Now I wish I had some of my own. Sometimes I want very much to get married.

"It really *is* funny. There was one-time — just before you came to New York — I nearly did marry Pete. But it wasn't love — it was just loneliness. I went up to Vassar to speak before their Civic Club during Commencement Week. I'd never known I was sentimental before. But, one night — well, the Five Year Class was having its reunion on the campus. They had a sheet up between two trees. The committee had had magic lantern slides made from the photographs of the girls' families. And each girl had to get up when her pictures were thrown on the screen and make a speech — introducing her family to the others.

"Of course it wasn't my class. I didn't know any of the girls. I sat out on the fringe of the crowd and watched. Some of the girls' were silly and the speeches they made about their husbands and children were sickening. One girl was already a widow and broke down completely when her husband's picture appeared. But most of them had — or pretended to have — joyous stories to tell. Each married woman seemed very proud of 'her man.' They were condescendingly superior to their classmates who hadn't married.

"And somehow — well — it got my nerve. It made me — sitting there by myself — appallingly lonely. It frightened me. Here was I, from the marrying point of view, letting my best years go to waste. I had a terrifying picture of myself as a lonely old maid — nobody caring for me — a cat and all that. And the babies in those lantern pictures looked very wonderful.

"Well, I had to catch the earliest train in the morning so it wasn't worth while going to bed. I sat up what was left of the night out on the campus, under the trees. I almost made up my mind to marry Pete. If he'd only known what was going on inside of me then, he might have had me."

"You speak — almost regretfully."

"No, not at all! As I said, it was only loneliness. Pete missed his chance and I got over it. It was a strange sentimental fit that came and went. It wasn't Pete. Why, I'd have almost married a police-man that morning — or the black Pullman porter — any one who asked me: I was so lonely. It wasn't love. No, not at all! It would have been awful if I'd married Pete."

"So," Eunice summed it up, "you don't want him, but you do want to marry somebody?"

Helen nodded an unenthusiastic assent.

"It isn't quite so simple as that," she said. "Mar-riage in the abstract doesn't smile to me especially. That fit of loneliness passed. I'm not afraid of the future. But I would like to care for some one — really love some one."

"Well, then," Eunice said, "I hope Pete disap-pears."

Helen looked a question.

"It would give Win a chance. He thinks you're en-gaged to Pete."

"Oh, pooh!" Helen sniffed. "Win doesn't care for me — not that way."

"Win's fine," Eunice said.

"Yes. A fine friend."

"But you said you did not believe men and women could be friends."

"That was foolishness. I was discouraged — thinking of Pete. Win's different."

Eunice did not look convinced.

It was something of a shock to Eunice when Pete dropped in to dinner one night a week or ten days after this talk. He was unchanged, as merry, as un-concerned as ever. It was more of a shock to her to

see that Helen accepted the renewal of diplomatic relations as though nothing had happened.

In this matter Helen was obviously less decisive,
less sure of herself, than usual.

For more than four years — and it had been going
on before she came to New York — Eunice watched,
with acute curiosity, this strange friendship between
Helen and Pete. She could see no progress, no " getting anywhere." It became her regular little joke,
whenever Helen looked depressed, to ask: " Has Pete
been spoiling things again?" Generally Helen
nodded a gloomy assent.

In the spring of 1913, Pete became suddenly and
noticeably rarefied. He explained that he was very
busy in Albany. He was seldom in the city and rarely
stayed overnight when he came. As much as three
weeks would pass without his appearing at the Flat.

" Is he really getting tired at last? " Eunice asked
herself. " Or is he trying to make Helen miss him? "
She watched her friend closely, but could see no indication of her feeling. Early in September the news
exploded that Pete was engaged to a Miss Grace
Caldwell, the daughter of a State senator in Albany.
Helen was the only one of the friends who took the
news calmly. She said that she had known for a long
time. But it was weeks before she would talk to
Eunice about it. She had never been so uncommuni-
cative before, and at last Eunice, unable to stand
the silence longer, asked Helen if she knew the girl.

" Oh, yes, slightly. She's a little ' pink face,' a
Dresden doll effect —' nobody home ' sort of person
— utterly stupid. Her mother tries to be the

Madam Roland of the Progressives — tries to run a political salon. Every one laughs at her and Grace is worse — just out of finishing school. I'm sick about it."

Still Helen seemed reluctant to talk and changed the subject; but, after Eunice was in bed, she came and sat with her a while.

" Of course everybody thinks I'm jealous," she said, " but I'm not. God knows I could have married him, if I'd wanted to. But I can't help feeling bad about it. Perhaps it's a good thing for him. He seems pleased. Perhaps I ought to rejoice with him, but I can't, she seems such a fool. In a way I suppose I am jealous — just as Win is so jealous of Lillian. It means losing a friend, the best friend I ever had. Grace and I could never be friends — and besides, Pete, like a fool, told her that he'd been in love with me. She's afraid I'll try to pry him loose! She'd raise a horrible squawk, if she should hear that I was having lunch with him. No, he's a total loss, no hope of salvage. And he has meant so much to me."

Helen could think of no more to say on the subject and went dejectedly to bed.

So the Fates had dealt with Eunice. An ogre held her captive in a grim tower. She could look out through the grated windows of her narrow cell on the people outside, who were engaged in the real processes of living, and from time to time they brought her stories of their adventures in the great open spaces beyond her sight. In West Newleigh she had lived mostly in the children; here, in New York, she lived through Helen and her friends. Her contact with most of what is the reality of our life, had always been indirect and secondhand.

Into this world of hers, the Stranger — from a world so different — wandered in the week before Thanksgiving in the year 1913.

CHAPTER VI

THE FLAT

Helen had fitted up a workroom for herself in the apartment she shared with Eunice. Her regular office was in the Charities Building on Fourth Avenue. But often when she did not want to be disturbed by the routine work of directing her staff, she spent the afternoon at home and there she sometimes made appointments.

On the Thursday, after the Stranger had been introduced at Win's breakfast party, she was sitting in this private office with Mrs. van Loo, the president of "The Association for the Aid of Tubercular Children." She was refusing the proffered position as financial secretary of the Association.

Mrs. van Loo was a large woman. She would have looked motherly if she had not been so elaborately and expensively gotten up to appear young.

"The board authorized me," she said, "to offer you thirty-five hundred. But we want you very much. I think — this is unofficial, of course — but I think we might arrange four thousand."

"It isn't the salary, Mrs. van Loo," Helen said. "I couldn't honorably throw up my present job till the work is well organized. And I'm promised to the National Housing Association as soon as I'm free.

I'm hopelessly tied up. But I know just the person for you — Mr. Yates. I picked him out when I first joined the Child Labor Committee as an able fellow. He's been my right-hand man ever since. I don't like to lose him, but I can't pay him more than two thousand and he's worth more. You couldn't do better."

Eunice, dressed in her street clothes, opened the door of the Flat and came down the hall past Helen's little office.

"Oh, Eunice," Helen called, and then to her guest, "excuse me a minute, I have a message for my roommate, Miss Bender."

"Is it Eunice Bender, the artist? Oh, I'd so like to know her."

"Eunice, let me introduce you to Mrs. van Loo."

"I'm so glad to meet you!" Mrs. van Loo said effusively. "You've no more devoted admirers than my children, I'm sure. When I tell them I've seen you, they'll be wild with excitement. And do you write the verses, too? They're so fine for children, they're so easily learned. My three know dozens of them by heart. And — the funny things — they're always asking me to get them a new little brother like Little Tot. But I think three are quite enough for a busy woman. Don't you? Too much I think sometimes."

Mrs. van Loo's talk was so fast that it gathered great momentum and drove past commas and question-marks and periods without noticing them.

"And there's no one, Miss Bender, who does more to bring joy to my larger brood of crippled children.

In every children's hospital in the city, they know
Tit and Tot and all of them. You'll have a new book
for this Christmas, won't you? And, oh, I wonder if
you could make a Christmas card for me? Especially
for the little cripples — something about Tit, Tat,
Toe, and Little Tot coming to visit them in the hospital — and Santa Claus? I could have them printed
and sent with my presents to the poor kiddies. And
if you could only go the rounds with me some day.
You'd be surprised to find how they all know your
name. It would make them so happy. Would you?"

Eunice was very tired and noticeably pale. This
vehement unparagraphed discourse winded her. But
she leaned up against the door jamb and smiled
valiantly.

"I'll do the Christmas card for you, Mrs. van Loo.
I'm glad the youngsters like my work. But I'm
afraid I can't visit the hospitals with you. I'm not
any too strong myself."

"No," Helen said, "Eunice isn't up to that. She
has to be very careful."

"Oh, I'm so sorry to hear it. You don't look very
well to-day. I hope it's not serious —"

Mrs. van Loo went on in voluble and vacuous sympathy. She really was sorry, but it did not sound so.
She had sympathized with sick people too often to
do it convincingly. Such talk was always painful to
Eunice, so she interrupted.

"I've been fighting with my publishers this afternoon and I'm very tired — so I'm afraid you'll have
to excuse me.— Helen, can I speak to you just a
moment? — I'll do the Christmas card for you, Mrs.

van Loo, and don't forget to give my love to the children."

"No, indeed. They'll be so pleased. I'm very glad to have met you. I *do* hope you'll be better soon."

Helen walked out in the hallway with Eunice.

"I'm all in. Tell Jennie to bring me some tea and toast for supper — in bed."

"Oh, Eunice, do you have to go to bed? That Mr. Lane is coming in to talk about costumes for Thanksgiving. Lillian telephoned that she would bring him over about nine."

Eunice considered this a moment.

"Well, I'll lie down till dinner time anyhow."

"To get back to business, Mrs. van Loo," Helen said, as she rejoined her guest. "I can very cordially recommend this Mr. Yates. You see, I've practically brought ——"

"Does Miss Bender ever do portraits of children? I'd like to have her paint mine. They'd love it."

"I never knew her to do portraits, but I'll ask her. As I was saying, I've practically brought up Mr. Yates. I've trained him. I know the people available for such work and you can't do better. Twenty-five hundred would be a fair salary to start him on."

For a few minutes they haggled over terms.

"Brains cost money in charity, just as they do in business," Helen said, "but they more than pay for themselves. He'll double your income."

And so, at last, it was arranged.

As soon as the door had closed on Mrs. van Loo, Helen went to Eunice's room.

"I'm tired, too," she said, tumbling onto the foot

of the bed. "My! That van Loo woman is a scatter-
brain. Can't keep her mind on one subject ten
seconds. By the way, she wants to know if you'd
paint her children."

"Not if they're as noisy as she is!"

Eunice was stretched out on her bed. She put her
hands over her eyes. Plainly she did not want to
talk. The sight of physical suffering always distressed Helen, she would have much preferred to slip
away. But she was convinced that solitary medita-
tion on her ills — what Dr. Riggs called "moping"—
was the very worst thing for Eunice. And persist-
ence, insistence, had been the formula of Helen's success as a social-service financier.

"What were you fighting with your publishers
about?" she asked.

Eunice, having learned from long experience that
it was easier to submit to Helen's determinations,
pulled herself together to reply. They talked about
contracts and royalties, about Mr. Yates and Mrs. van
Loo till it was time to dress for dinner.

When, later in the evening, the doorbell announced
the arrival of Lillian and Mr. Lane, Eunice, in a soft
clinging gown of blue and not looking tired any more,
was reading. Helen presented a striking contrast.
She wore a smart, crisp evening dress, which looked
starched but was not. A picture of spruceness and
health, she was sitting at the center table working
on a folio of business papers. She gathered them into
an orderly pile, but left them in plain sight as she
turned to welcome the guests.

"Oh, girls!" Lillian burst out. "Mr. Lane is per-

fectly wonderful! He can get all the costumes from
'The Caliph's Daughter.' It has just finished its
run."

"Are you connected with the theater, Mr. Lane?"
Helen asked.

Her question was so brusque that he started and
stammered. It would be hard to imagine a person
who had less of the assured Broadway look.

"Oh, no! But there were some Moors —'supers'
in the play — from the Anghera Hills. I did some
interpreting for them. There was no one at the
French consulate who knew their dialect. They were
quite bewildered — caused a good deal of trouble to
the management — till they found some one to speak
for them."

"That's the best part of it," Lillian said, with grow-
ing enthusiasm. "He knows those people. The
musicians and acrobats. He says some of them can
cook — give us a real Persian supper."

"Moroccan," Lane protested.

"And the property man," Lillian ignored the cor-
rection, "is going to lend us the tent from the third
act — it will fill about half of the Studio. And Mr.
Lane's Armenian friend has rugs and cushions and
everything. But the costumes are the best! You remember that wonderful creamy and scarlet gown with
the umbrella skirt? The Caliph's daughter wears it
in the second act. He's going to get that for me!"

She did not wait for the applause this drew to die
down.

"And that black and gold thing the favorite wife
wears in the finale — you'd look stunning in that,

Helen! It would just about fit. And for Eunice—
I can't quite make up my mind. Frank says the old
gold dress — the one the girl who recites the prologue
wore — would suit you best. But I can never see
why you wear old gold. I should think with your hair
you'd choose more of a contrast. But it don't matter.
You can have whatever you want. There are heaps of
costumes for you and Irene to pick from. Isn't it
gorgeous?"

Lane was pleased that they were pleased. He tried
to enter intelligently into these discussions of dresses,
but was plainly in deep water. However he was
quite definite in siding with Frank about Eunice's
costume. He was sure that the gown of old gold
would be becoming.

"And if you want the feast to be really Oriental,"
he said, "we must have a story-teller. There is a
very good one with this troupe. He can't speak
English, but I could interpret."

"Won't all this cost a good deal, Mr. Lane?"
Eunice asked. "You must promise to let us all share
the expense equally."

"It will cost very little. I could not pay the Moors,
if I tried. They are all foolishly grateful. I only
went up to the theater now and then to smooth out
their difficulties. It was not much, and I found it
interesting. But they think it was a great deal.
They will be glad to do it for me."

"Well, if that's so," Helen said, "let's have the
dancing girls, too. They're so typical."

"I am afraid we had better not ask them," Lane
said.

He blushed slightly, in evident confusion at her suggestion. Helen did not like opposition.

"I don't see why not."

"Really," Lane stammered in embarrassment, "I — well — you see, the men, the musicians, they would think — well — in their country such girls only dance before men — not before ladies."

"But here," Helen persisted, "they do it every night."

"It does not matter what they think of the women in the audiences. But I would not like to have them think ill of the ladies I know — as they do of the women who come to public places to see vulgar dances."

"What rubbish!" Helen snorted. "I suppose they think we're abandoned hussies because we don't wear veils"

"Oh, no!" he said, quite seriously. "They think it is a strange custom not to wear veils. They think your men cannot care much for you — to let you be seen so by all the world. But they are wise enough to know that there must be many chaste women in any country — even among the naked black folk of Africa."

This rather overwhelmed Helen. It almost silenced her, but she could not forego a last word.

"I don't see why we have to worry about their silly prejudices," she said.

"I'll arrange it, if I can," Lane said, bowing submissively.

Further discussion of this point was averted by the arrival of Lancaster.

"Seeing you saves writing a note," Lillian said as the greeting subsided. "We're going to have a Persian dinner on Thanksgiving night. And we're counting on you and Irene. Mr. Lane is arranging the costumes for us."

"All right," Lancaster said, rather ruefully at the idea of such frivolity. "I suppose Irene will want to come."

And then, having had his own reason for coming to the Flat, he went directly to it.

"I've just been around to your rooms, Mr. Lane. As you weren't there, I looked in on Mathews, found Frank there. He said you were here. I've wanted to get acquainted, ever since Inslavsky ran off with you last Sunday. I'm very much interested in the Revolution in Russia. I heard him call you 'Tovarish'— and that means 'comrade.' Tell us about it. How did you meet Inslavsky?"

Lane evidently was reluctant to answer. He glanced about from one to another as if looking for help.

"Perhaps you had better ask Inslavsky. I do not know — I am not sure that he would want me to tell. I was only in Russia a short time. I do not know much about the Revolution. Inslavsky could tell you so much more than I."

He was more embarrassed than ever by the awkward silence. Eunice came to his rescue with some small talk about costumes. They discussed plans for Thanksgiving until Lillian left with Mr. Lane.

"He's a queer person," Lancaster said to the two girls. "He can't be much interested in the Revolution — or he'd be in touch with the comrades here and know that he didn't have to distrust us.

"I heard a great yarn about him yesterday. I was up at Cambridge arranging for Inslavsky's speech to the students. I had lunch with Petroff, he's to preside at our meeting and he's head of the Department of Semitic Languages. He knows Lane — discovered him in fact. It's a weird story.

"Last year Petroff went to Morocco on the trail of some Arabic manuscripts. When the Moors were driven out of Spain they took their books with them. And up at Morocco City, the old capital, Petroff succeeded in getting admission to the library of the university — it was a famous school in the old days. And there he found a native scholar, named Kassim, who knew all about the manuscripts. After talking Arabic for a couple of weeks, this 'native scholar' began to speak English and turned out to be Lane. Petroff says he was born out there — the son of a missionary. He dressed and lived like the natives — passed himself off as a Mohammedan. But as soon as he found out that Petroff was really in earnest, really knew his subject, he became quite friendly.

"Petroff says he knows more about Arabic and kindred languages than any white man alive. He tried at once to get him to come to America. It seems that Lane did not want to come at first. Petroff used some queer bait to land him. There's a language called 'Shilah,' which the mountaineers speak in the High Atlas. It's an unwritten language, so it's hard to study and nobody knows much about it. But Lane knew it well. It seems that a German faker had made a great stir among Orientalists by publishing a Shilah grammar. It was all wrong — a bluff. It made Lane so angry, when Petroff showed it to him, that he came to America — on the Harvard Oriental Fund — to publish a true grammar. Petroff says it's the most important contribution to comparative philology that's been made in decades — clears up a number of obscure points about the relations between Phœnician, Hebrew, Arabic, and other Semitic languages.

"When Lane finished the grammar he came here to New York to work for the Oriental Society. He's getting out an anthology of Shilah folklore and poetry. Petroff is enthusiastic about him — says that at last America has an Orientalist to be proud of. And it's strange — he never told Petroff that he'd been in Russia.

"It makes me sore to think that he's been living here, within easy reach, and I didn't know him. I could get so much from him for my book on 'Coöperation among Primitive Peoples.' A man can't know so much about languages without knowing a good deal about ethnology. I —"

"I'm afraid I'll have to go to bed," Eunice interrupted; "I'm awfully tired."

As she got up from the couch, she staggered slightly and went pale. Lancaster jumped up to steady her.

"It's nothing," she said, "a little vertigo. I'm all right — only tired." And shaking off his hand, she walked with fair steadiness to the door. "Good night."

"Is she worse?" Lancaster asked.

Helen shrugged her shoulders in perplexity.

"I don't know. I'm afraid so. You'd best run along, so I can help her to bed."

And when she had let Lancaster out, she went quickly to Eunice's room.

"I'm afraid you oughtn't to have stayed up," she said.

"Oh, Helen, dear. Please! Don't you suppose I know I oughtn't to have stayed up? Don't rub it in!"

And Helen knew, from the petulance of Eunice's voice, that she was unusually tired.

CHAPTER VII

THANKSGIVING

One end of the Studio was hung with an imitation camel's hair tent. There were divans on three sides and a wealth of stage-property cushions sprinkled here and there with real ones from the Armenian's curio shop. There was an arabesque cloth hung like a wainscoting about the angle of honor. And on the floor was a wonderful Atli rug of soft blues and old rose tints, which Lane had brought from his rooms. A canvas drop curtain, painted after the Bokhara design, but much larger than any real Bokhara rug, hung across the room before the open end of the tent and shut off the bare half of the Studio.

Beyond this curtain, a group of Moors squatted on the floor about some earthenware stoves, where, over glowing charcoals, some strangely smelling foods were cooking. Lillian, who, in spite of the sumptuous costume of the Caliph's Daughter, looked anything but Oriental, was watching them.

"Is everything ready?" she asked a Moorish *taleb* in flowing white, who, in spite of his ready English, did not at all resemble the Lane of American clothes.

"Just a minute," he replied. He gave some final directions in the guttural dialect of the Anghera Hills.

"All right," he said. "We will bring them in."

He pulled aside the imitation rug and they passed into the space before the tent.

"Oh! It's beautiful," Lillian said gleefully.

"I supose it is the best we can do here. But those Japanese lanterns with the electric lights ——"

"Candles," she interrupted with finality, "would be too dangerous."

She opened the door into the parlor.

The merriment which had sounded through stopped suddenly. Lane bent low as the guests entered, welcoming them with the Arabic greeting —"*Salaam aleikum*"—"peace be upon you."

"Oh!"—"Ah!"—"Fine!"

"Where's Mr. Lane?" Helen asked.

"That's him — he bowed you in," Lillian laughed.

They all turned and looked at Lane, who, in real Moorish clothes, did not begin to come up to their idea of Oriental gorgeousness. Among their stage costumes he looked rather like a field daisy mixed up in a chrysanthemum show.

"Let us sit down," he said, awkward as usual, when he felt himself the center of attention.

Win, remembering how the Caliph did it in the theater, shook off his slippers as he stepped on the fine old Atli rug. Lane did so as second nature. The others, noticing them, followed suit, with much merriment.

"I suppose we ought to sit down cross-legged," Helen said.

"Oh, be comfortable," Lane urged. "That is why we have so many cushions."

A grinning little black boy about ten years old,

with a red fez cocked rakishly on one side of his shaven head, came in from behind the curtain with an elaborately chased brass bowl for hand-washing. Lane called it a "*tass*." He washed first to show them how, and then, one after another, they held out their hands and little black Ahmed poured on them the warm, rose-scented water.

He removed the *tass* and returned with a low, round table laden with tea things and set it down before Lockwood.

"What do I do with this?" he asked.

"Oh! The host always makes the tea — it is the strictest etiquette. You see the traditional way to get rid of your enemies is to poison their tea. If the host seemed anxious to make it, the guests would be afraid. So you must urge each of us to make it — to reassure us. But it would be very rude for any of us to accept the task — it would show that we did not trust you. So in the end the host always makes it."

"But I don't know how," Frank said. ". We'll have to trust you."

"Not a very cheerful custom," Irene said, "begin- ning a meal with the fear you may be poisoned." Long association with children in the capacity of teacher had given her an assertive, positive manner of speech. "I wouldn't like the East. I suppose there's a frightful lot of dirt. Fancy! Eating with one's hands!"

"Yes," Lane admitted. "There is a greal deal of dirt — not the kind you are used to here."

"That's one on you, Irene," Lancaster laughed.

"When we think of New York City and all the filth of the slums — where the great mass of our people live — we haven't any right to throw stones. We've an East of our own — the East Side."

Lane was afraid it would hurt Miss Penton's feelings to be laughed at.

"I did not mean to make a joke," he said. "But I do not think it any dirtier to eat with your fingers, which you have just washed, than with a fork, which a careless servant has washed — perhaps. And going into a house with your shoes on — after walking in the street. You are accustomed to that and it does not seem dirty to you — but of course it is. It shocks us."

Little Ahmed, coming in to remove the tea outfit, addressed Lane in Arabic. Win pricked up his ears.

"What did he call you?"

"Hadji Kassim — that's my Moorish name."

"But 'Hadji' is a religious title, isn't it?" Win asked. "I thought it meant a person who had been on the pilgrimage. Have you been to Mecca?"

"Yes."

"Have you, indeed?" Lancaster exclaimed. "I want to hear about that some time. I've read Sir Richard Burton's account of his trip to Mecca. But aren't these people angry about it? I thought they were very bitter against any outsider going to their holy cities."

"But I'm not an outsider. I'm a believer — a Mohammedan."

"You don't wear a fez," Lancaster said.

Lane was embarrassed, not by the cross-questioning,

but by having to talk of himself. He tried to turn the conversation lightly.

" I don't believe God cares what fashion of hats we wear."

" This interests me," Lancaster persisted. " I thought the Muslims were very fanatical about such things."

" Some of them are — just like some Christians. Not very many years ago they burned people at the stake in Russia over the question of whether the priest should make the sign of the cross with three fingers or with the thumb and two fingers. There are foolish fanatics everywhere. But I am quite sure that God is not a foolish fanatic. Do you not agree with me? "

" Now, for an argument," Win said dolefully. " Lancaster doesn't believe in any God."

Ahmed caused an ineffectual diversion by bringing in a steaming dish of *kous-kous-soo*. There was a pyramid of white meal, its sides inlaid with a formal design of carrots and beets, with a stewed chicken atop.

" Defend your lack of faith, Lancaster," Win said teasingly.

Lancaster did not want to alienate Lane by making fun of his beliefs, but he could not resist Win's challenge.

" You really believe in God? "

" Yes," Lane said quite simply. " In my God — Allah. Not in the God of the Jews, who sits on a throne — a man-god with ' a right hand,' who got vexed at his creatures and cried over their sins, drowned them in a flood òf his tears — cried, as the Jewish books say, till his eyes were sore. Not in the Christian God — who had a son.''

" You won't find many people nowadays,'' Win said, "who believe in the anthropomorphic — man-god — with hands and feet and sore eyes.''

" I don't believe in any kind of a God,'' Lancaster said, " with or without sore eyes.''

" Nor I,'' Helen put in.

" Are you not sorry sometimes? '' Lane asked. " I would be. I do not suppose any one can believe in God all the time. We have to stop to sleep and eat and do so many little things. But it is very good to believe in God when you can spare the time.''

" Well,'' Eunice said, to steer out of the argument, "let's stop philosophizing and eat a little. Do you eat this, too, with your hands? ''

" Yes. And *kous-kous-soo* has its etiquette, too. No matter how clever your disguise, nor how well you spoke his language, you could not fool a Moor, unless you know how to eat *kous-kous-soo*. First, the host pulls off a piece of meat like this and offers it to the most honored guest, who sits at his right. I will offer it to you, Miss Bender — as you are at my right — so. And the host says — ' *Bis-m-illah* '—' In the Name of God '— a blessing. And you must say — ' *El-hamdu-l-illah* '—' Praise be to God '—a thanksgiving. And you must take it with your right hand — the left hand is an insult. Then every one takes a handful of meal — like this. You can make a ball of it — see. Try it,— no. It is difficult. It takes much practice. We will have spoons. *Ahmed!* ''

"It certainly tastes good," Win said.

"What do the poor people eat in Morocco?" Lancaster asked.

"Oh, everybody eats *kous-kous-soo*. The rich Kaïds, of course, will have chicken with it — or a piece of meat. The common people have to be content with partridges or quails."

"What a topsy-turvy land," Eunice laughed. "You have to be very rich here to have game birds."

"With us, the boys catch them in snares. They don't cost anything."

While they were eating the *kous-kous-soo*, an orchestra of four pieces appeared. One had a small, tall drum, which he beat with his hands. There was a reed flute and a " ginbri," a minute sort of mandolin. The fourth musician had a "*r'bab*," the instrument on which Win had heard Lane play. The four men, after bowing to the company, stood up, held out their hands as if holding the Holy Book, and recited a verse, from the Koran.

"What's that?" Eunice asked.

"The Fatihah — like your Lord's Prayer. Only it is all thanksgiving — not begging bread. I will translate it.

> "Praise be to God, the Lord of all creatures,
> The most Compassionate of the Merciful,
> King of the Day of Judgment,
> Thee do we worship and of Thee do we ask guidance.
> Lead us in the True Path,
> In the way of those on whom is Thy Grace,
> Not in the Path of the unrighteous
> Nor in that of those who have gone astray."

"You see," he said, "it is a prayer of praise —
and this is your Thanksgiving Day. Now they will
sing a '*keemjad*'— an address of welcome."

While they were singing, Ahmed brought in a cas-
serole —lamb, stewed in oil, with seeded grapes and
olives. He was very awkward in handing·about the
knives and forks. He did not know how, and Irene,
who was squeamish in such matters, noticed with
horror that as often as not he picked up a knife by
the blade — in his black fingers. She decided that
after all there was something to be said on behalf of
eating with one's own hands.

Frank dished out a plateful and handed it to Helen.

"What is it I should say?" he asked.

"*Bis-m-illah.*"

"And I?" Helen asked.

"*El-hamu-l-illah.*"

"What do you call this dish?" Irene asked.

"*Tajeen.*"

"I must say," she said, "I like their cooking better
than their music. This *tajeen* is as delicious as the
noise is discordant."

"It is not really discordant," Lane protested,
"only your ear is not used to such fine shades. You
have made all your music rigid to fit your piano —
the octave — everything just alike. You could not
play that on your piano. There are twelve intervals
equal to your eight."

"I don't catch so many."

"No?"

He took the *r'bab* from the player and asked Irene
to give him the scale.

"Good!" he said, as she sang the do, re, mi. He struck the high and low c. "Now, listen."

He ran up the duodecimal scale. Handing the instrument back he spoke a few words of Arabic to the performers.

"They will sing the Hamadsha funeral chant. It isn't meant for instruments. You can get so much more delicate tonic value out of strings than you can from the voice. It is a chant. The marching song of those who carry the coffin. It is in one of the Gregorian modes. Your ears will catch the tones."

The voices of the musicians did not have the timbre to which we are accustomed, and the rhythm, especially the weird insistence of the drum, was unusual, but the melody was octaval and enough like our own to allow its peculiar beauty to be felt by Western ears. "Why," Win said, "there's a movement to that which sounds like Handel."

"Yes," Irene admitted, "that's better. Much!"

"It sounds like a song of victory," Eunice said.

"Well, with us, we look on death as a sort of victory."

Ahmed, who had taken away the *tajeen*, came back with the *tass*, and when they had washed their hands again, he brought in a tablecloth, held up by the four corners like a bag, and threw it open on the rug. There was an amazing potpourri of white cookies, oranges, nuts, bananas, cranberries, tuberoses, and carnations.

Ahmed came again with a censer of frankincense, which he swung about till the tent was heavy with the pungent and exquisite scent. Then with a bundle of fragrant grasses he sprinkled them with rose water from a silver bowl.

The orchestra struck up a " Streets of Cairo " tune and a slim and graceful dancer, barefooted, in gaudy, electric blue silk trousers, a red sash and burnt orange bodice, hung with heavy, clanking silver jewelry — anklets, bracelets, ponderous earrings — clattered into the space before the tent and began the *danse du ventre*. Whether the dancer's face was pretty or not, it was quite impossible to tell. It was overlaid, almost masked, with paint, scarlet lips, a spot of carmine on each cheek, the eyebrows heavily exaggerated with antimony.

Helen from the other side of the tent nodded a " thank you " to Lane.

"I thought you weren't going to bring a girl," Eunice whispered.

"Do not tell," he replied, winking slyly. " It is a boy. I had a hard time persuading him to dress up like a girl and dance before women. Do not tell Miss Cash. . She would be disappointed."

When the dance was finished, Ahmed brought in a wide brass tray, covered with tiny cups of coffee and cigarettes. An old, white-bearded, venerable, wizened Moor in an immense turban came in and bowed profoundly. Lane rose to return his salutation respectfully and offered him a cigarette, which he lighted for him.

"Ladies and gentlemen," he said, " allow me to present Sidi Bobker bin Abd-el-Khader Azroor. He is a professional troubadour and story-teller. No Moorish banquet would be complete without some stories, so I have invited Sidi Bobker. Of course the best of his stories are too long for me to translate without tiring you. I have asked him for short ones.

"And, with your permission, I will ask the other Moors, who have been serving us, to come and listen. It is the custom — and they enjoy it very much."

Little black Ahmed, who was Sidi Bobker's slave, produced an immense tambourine, nearly three feet across, and, squatting down on his heels, beat a most intricate tattoo. The other Moors — including the lad, who had danced and who had quickly washed the shame from his face and had put on again the garb of manhood — sat about in a semicircle. Lane threw them handfuls of the mixed dessert and cigarettes.

When all were in place, Ahmed stopped his racket. Sidi Bobker stood up, spread out his hands in the attitude of prayer, recited the Fatihah, and invoked the blessing of his patron saint, Sidi L'mdoog.

The Moors roared with laughter as the old man told his tale. A queer glint came into Lane's eyes. It was a mixture of embarrassment and of amusement. Sidi Bobker had no sooner started, than Lane had realized that he could not translate this story. He knew enough of American life to understand that such droll tales could not be told to ladies — except in intimate privacy. Although thinking hard to escape the embarrassment of the situation, he was mightily amused at the contrast in conventionalities. Sidi Bobker, who disapproved of unveiled women to such an extent that he would not look at their faces, was blissfully unconscious of any indelicacy in describing their more intimate charms.

"I am sorry," Lane said, when the story was finished. "It is impossible to translate. All the wit of it is in play upon words. Although you do not like puns, my people are very fond of them. Anyhow puns lose their point when translated! But please laugh a little so the old man's feelings will not be hurt. He would think me very stupid, if he knew I could not translate."

Luckily a slow-witted Moor suddenly caught the point of one of Sidi Bobker's jests and exploded in a roar of laughter which was infectious.

"I will ask him for another story," Lane said. "We will hope for better luck this time."

Sidi Bobker bowed in acknowledgment of the compliment implied in the request for another effort. Little Ahmed made the tambourine roar for a moment and the old man began again.

"*Ay! Ay! El-hamdu-l-illah!*" the Moors ejaculated in solemn approval.

"This is not a funny story," Lane said, as he began his translation. "It is — well — religious.

"In the land of Makaïnfaïn, which means in the land of nowhere — like your 'Once upon a time' — there lived a poet, Khamedo, and he loved a maiden named, after the Prophet's wife, Khadijah — on her be the peace and favor of Allah.

"One evening the young man, Khamedo, went to the house where Khadijah dwelt alone. He knocked on the door. The voice of his beloved answered:

"'Who is there?'

"'It is I.'

"'There is no room within but for one.'

"Khamedo went apart into the mountains to consider this hard saying. For many years he wandered
over the face of the earth seeking wisdom. He made
the Hadj, he visited the holy shrines of Irak and
Turkestan. And everywhere he sang praise of the
beauty and virtue of Khadijah. He made her fame
resound in the four great courts of Islam and even in
the lands of the Unbelievers. After many hardships
by hill country and plain, by desert and sea, he returned to his own country. He was worn by his
wayfaring — rich only in wisdom.

"He went once more to the house where Khadijah
dwelt alone. He knocked on the door and once more
the voice of his beloved asked:

"'Who is there?'

"And he answered:

"'I am Love, I am thou. We three be One.'

"And his Beloved opened the door — for truly the
water and the cup and the drinker are One."

"I don't see the point of that," Irene said, as Lane
dropped his voice, evidently at the end of the story.
"What has the water and the cup to do with it?"

"That is only another way of saying that Love and
the Lover and the Beloved are One. It is a mystic
formula — an emphasis on Monotheism. It is a
typical Eastern story in its attitude toward Love.
Khadijah would not open her door to the individual
Khamedo, but she welcomed Love. The man had no
significance by himself — as a person; it was the
Love he brought which she welcomed, to which she
opened her heart. She welcomed the chance to approach, through Love, the Oneness, which is God."

"It's too deep for me," Helen said.

"It is strange," Lane continued. "Evidently this story does not appeal to you. But it is one of the most popular in Sidi Bobker's repertoire — for my people. To us, the principal ills of life come from our separateness — our 'individuality,' as you call it. We suffer because we are isolated — exiled from God's Oneness. And Love is most wonderful, because it offers escape from this separateness, this home-sickness — this imprisonment in our little selves. Love leads out from ourself to another and so brings us nearer to the ultimate Unity. You Westerners love people, and we, loving Love, are grateful to the person who stirs Love within us. It is a deeply re-ligious idea to us.

"One of our poets, Jami, the Persian, has said:

"'Drink deep of earthly love, so will thy lip
The wine of Heaven's vintage learn to sip.'

And Abou Saïd, also a Persian, a greater man and a greater poet than Omar, has a rubaiya in the same strain. It is something like this:

"'O Most Beauteous One,' I asked, 'to whom dost thou belong?'
She replied to me, saying, 'To myself alone. For I am One.
Equally am I the Love, the Lover and the Beloved.
Alike am I the mirror, the beauty and the vision.'

"Of course those are poor translations of an idea which is common and very beautiful to us. We can-not understand your——"

The doorbell, ringing lustily, interrupted him. Frank got up amid protests.

"Don't let any one in."

"We don't want to be disturbed."

But Frank shook his head hopelessly as he came back.

"It's a young man in a fez," he said. "He doesn't speak English very well. I couldn't take his message. I guess you'll have to talk to him, Lane. He mentioned the Persian consulate."

Lane went out in the parlor to talk with the interrupter.

"I'm so sorry," he said, when he returned. "It seems to be my fate to be always taken away. A poor man is in trouble. Perhaps I can help him. I must go"— and then to Lillian —"it has been most kind of you, Mrs. Lockwood, to include me, who am a stranger, in your Thanksgiving celebration. I have enjoyed it very much — knowing you all. I thank you."

"Thanking us!" Frank protested. "Why, we're no end obliged to you. We all thank you for this treat. We're sorry you must go. What shall I do with these chaps? Can they find their way home alone?"

"I will tell them."

"And thank them for us, please," Eunice said. "We are sorry you have to leave. But we'll see you again."

"Thanks."

After giving directions to the Moors and telling Lillian that he would come back in the morning to help her clear up, he thanked them all again and said "good night."

CHAPTER VIII

THE NEXT MORNING

The next morning about eight, Helen, in her dressing gown, a newspaper under her arm, tiptoed to
Eunice's door and silently pushed it open.

"How are you this morning?"

Eunice always dreaded the question. She disliked
to lie and she disliked to admit her ill feelings. She
shrugged her shoulders under the bedclothes.

"Are you too tired?" Helen insisted.

"Oh, no. Just very tired. I don't sleep it off
as easily as most. I'll be all right. What's the
news?"

"News? Our friend, Mr. Lane, has a column and
a half in the newspaper."

"Not about us?"

"No. He didn't tell where he'd been. Here it
is — the headlines — '*Arabian Nights Entertainment
in Jefferson Market — the grimness of the Night
Court touched with Oriental color.*' I'll skip the first
part — it's supposed to be a funny story. It seems
that a man who couldn't speak English was brought
in for a row with a ticket chopper in the subway.
The regular interpreter thought he was Chinese. The
Chinese interpreter thought he was a Turk. The
Turkish interpreter said he was Persian. A man

125

came from the Persian consulate. He couldn't talk
with the prisoner, but said he knew a man who prob·
ably could and he set out to find Lane. I'll read: '

"'About midnight there was a craning of necks near the door
and in came an Oriental potentate in flowing white robes. He
was led up to the bar.

"'"Can he speak English?" Judge Black asked.

"'"Yes, your Honor," he answered for himself in the purest
English.

"'"What's your name?"

"'"Donald Lane."

"'"Why do you wear such outlandish clothes?"

"'"I have just come from a fancy dress party, your Honor.
Is it against the law?"

"'"Can you interpret for this man?"

"'"I do not know. I have not seen him."

"'"He's said to be a Persian. Can you speak Persian?"

"'"I can get along in three or four of the languages they
speak in Persia."

"'"Call up the defendant."

"'As soon as the poor chap was brought in — he was much
frightened, not knowing what it was all about — Mr. Lane spoke
up.

"'"He is not a Persian, your Honor. He is a Kirghese from
Turkestan. He is a Russian subject."

"'"Do you know his language?"

"'"Not well. But he probably speaks Tatar. Shall I try?"

"'"Tell him he is accused of disorderly conduct in the
Bleecker Street subway station."

"'At the first word in a language he understood the Kirghese
broke away from the policeman who was holding him, let out
a yell which was probably meant for joy, threw himself on the
floor, and began to kiss the hem of Mr. Lane's fancy dress.

"'"Tell him to stand up," the judge ordered.

"'Mr. Lane helped him to his feet and talked with him for a
minute.

"'"Come, come! We've wasted too much time over this case already," the judge said. "Is he guilty or not guilty?"

"'"He does not know what such words mean, your Honor. There was some misunderstanding over his ticket ——"

"'"He admits being in the subway station at the time mentioned in the complaint?"

"'"Naturally. That was where he was arrested?"

"'"Naturally won't do in law. I want to know whether he admits ——"

"'"Your Honor, he does not know the name of the station. He has told me already that he was in a station. There are two men here, the policeman and the subway guard who arrested him. If you cannot believe them, I will ask him to describe the station. But he is very much confused, your Honor. He does not understand why he was beaten."

"'"Oh, that's what they always say."

"'"That it happens often, your Honor, does not make it any easier for him to understand."

"'"He probably showed fight."

"'"Yes, of course. But he was unarmed — what could he do against four or five? He is too much excited to talk coherently. If you want the truth, let me take him into another room for a few minutes and I will get his story."

"'"That isn't regular procedure."

"'"Then, your Honor, I will have to let your regular interpreter attend to the case. I do not care to take part in the further prosecution of this man. He has not been proven guilty of anything. But he was beaten in the subway by the guard and a policeman, manhandled in the station house and again here."

"'"Well," Judge Black said, "I'll make an exception in his case. Take him into my chambers. See what you can do.'"

"Now, what do you think of that, Eunice? He's a queer fellow, isn't he? I never would have dreamed that he'd dare to talk back to a judge like that!"

"It doesn't surprise me," Eunice said. "I think

his embarrassed manner is due to us. He's not used
to women. But I don't think he'd be afraid of men.
How did the case turn out? "

"Oh, the judge discharged the man in Lane's cus-
tody. Of course it was all a mistake. He was a
horseback rider, come over from Buffalo Bill's show
— separated from his friends. You can read about
it after I'm gone. Will you have your coffee here?
Good! Stay in bed and get rested. I'll dress and
have mine in here with you."

Helen, leaving the paper, went to her room.
Eunice sat up, crammed some pillows behind her back,
and read about the Stranger, while Jenny, the Jamai-
can maid, brought in a little table and laid it beside
the bed. Soon Helen, dressed for her office, came
back. She poured out the coffee for both of them.

"This fellow Lané is certainly queer," she said,
"but he interests me."

"I like him."

For a moment they were silent and then Eunice
spoke again.

"While I've been lying here awake, I've been thinking about that story the old man told. And the more
you think about it, the better it is."

"It didn't make much of a hit with me. I don't
go in for this esoteric, mystic business. I've too
much to do, too many real things to attend to, to
waste time over such things. And Oriental love
stories — well, there's always something hothouse
about them — smell of the harem — polygamy and all
that."

"There wasn't anything polygamous about that

story," Eunice protested, "just the opposite, it struck me."

"Well, perhaps." Helen's mind was evidently on some other aspect of the case. " I don't know, but all that incense, the tuberoses, sort of went to my head, made me feel sickish. I didn't pay much attention to the story. It's too bad that he's so wrapped up in the East. If he'd had a more normal life, he might be a fine fellow."

" He wouldn't be so interesting, if he was just like everybody else."

" Why, you don't mean to say it's an advantage to be queer. It's an immense handicap."

" Perhaps."

" Certainly. Somebody ought to take him in hand and knock this Oriental nonsense out of him."

" Are you thinking of taking the job? "

" Me? " Helen asked with a start, then a laugh. " Oh, Lord, no. I'm too busy to take on any personal reformations. But, well, I might find a spare moment now and then. I'm sure he has a lot to him if it was only brought out. All he needs is a little steering. The queerest thing about his is his calling himself a Mohammedan! I can't help thinking that's a pose. It is hard enough nowadays to find educated people who really, honestly, believe in Christian theology. I can't imagine any intelligent person accepting all that Oriental superstition. I wonder where he found those queer collars. It would be a kindness for some one to point out to him that it doesn't pay to be queer. It's the worst reputation a person can have."

She looked to Eunice for confirmation. But
Eunice's eyes were closed. She felt a strange reluc-
tance to discuss Lane with Helen.

"It really would be a kindness," Helen insisted.

Eunice did not argue. And Helen went off to her
day's work.

Left alone, Eunice thought over Helen's threat of
reforming Lane. The worst of it was that in all their
long friendship, Helen had always succeeded in ac-
complishing what she set out to do.

"Why can't she leave him alone?" Eunice asked
herself.

When Helen had said, "He interests me," Eunice
had replied, "I like him." There was a vast difference between these two verdicts. There was also a
vast difference between the facts that while Helen
had hurried off to a very busy day in her office,
Eunice spent the morning in bed.

She thought over all her men friends. She needed
a standard by which to judge this Stranger. She did
not know many men well. All her friends were
secondhand. They had been Helen's first.

Best of all she liked Win. It was a red-letter day
for her when he called and Helen was out. Now and
then, when he knew she was sick, he would come and
sit by her bed. She enjoyed immensely his talk of
books and of his dreams. She knew he liked her.
And at times she had dreamed a tiny daydream about
what might have been if she had been well. Perhaps
if only she had been granted normal vitality, her
strong fondness for him might have developed into this
tumultuous thing about which books are written and

poems are sung. This was the nearest she had ever come to Romance. Never in all her life had she been able to escape from the fact that she was not well. It stood square in the way of so many "might have beens."

In some ways she felt even closer to Frank. He also liked her and came frequently to advise her about her work. Never but once had they talked together of fundamental things, but between them there was the fellowship of thwarted dreams. She had not been able to develop her talent beyond a children's toy. She, of all the group, saw most clearly into Frank's silent·tragedy. He also must have dreams to match his talent. There were his pictures in the Metropolitan and the Luxembourg. A few years ago there had been no painter in America with half his promise. But Lillian had stopped all that. It was not necessary for them to talk together. Now and then Eunice caught in his eyes an infinitely sad, far-away look — and understood. They each realized that the other's heart was not at all in the little tasks of everyday. They shared together homesickness for the Forests of Arden, the exile's longing to see again the Vale of Tempe, the heartbreak of those who have been excommunicated from the Rites of the Most Beautiful Goddess. But of such things we may not speak.

Lancaster, she respected highly, but his perpetual air of great occupations tired her. And Pete McGee, well, now that he was leaving Helen alone, Eunice missed his gay laugh. She had liked him more than she had thought.

But, quite definitely, she knew that she liked this Stranger better than any of them.

Why couldn't Helen leave him alone? The bitterest thought, as she lay there in bed, was the certainty that, if Helen set her mind to making him over according to her own specifications, she would succeed. She always did. And the reformation of Lane was the first of her projects in which Eunice did not wish her success. So generally had she approved of her friend's activities that Eunice was genuinely surprised at her own feeling in this matter — surprised to find herself longing to warn him, to urge him to escape before he fell into the toils.

Helen's mind, as she rode uptown to her office, was also preoccupied by the Stranger. Was it worth while for her to take a hand in his affairs? She rather thought it might be. And, it did not occur to her to doubt — any more than it did to Eunice — that she could succeed, if she set her mind to it. But once in her office, all thought of him was driven from her mind by the pile of work on her desk.

CHAPTER IX

THE STRANGER'S STORY

A few nights after Thanksgiving, Lane, as he was coming home to his rooms, noticed a light across the hall over Win's door. He hesitated a moment, as though considering a momentous question, and then knocked. The door was opened by Pete McGee, whom he had not seen before.

"Oh, I beg pardon," Lane said. "I wanted to see Mr. Mathews."

"Come in. He's here."

Lancaster was there, too. He had come to read the manuscript of the article Win had written about Inslavsky. They both jumped up to greet Lane.

"Glad to see you," Win said cordially.

"So am I," Lancaster chimed in. "When can one find you at home? I've knocked at your door a couple of times — but no answer."

"My name is McGee," Pete said. "These gentlemen with their accustomed politeness fail to introduce us, but I gather that you are Mr. Lane, the Man of Mystery."

"Yes. Lane is my name. I am glad to make your acquaintance. But I did not know I was a Man of Mystery."

"You didn't? Well, you don't realize your assets. Sit down. Have one of your estimable cigarettes —

we're all smoking them now. And I'll put the case to you.

"I've been playing around with this crowd for a dozen odd years. I go up to Albany for a few days and come back to find them all talking about a new-comer, who — count one — plays an outlandish musical instrument and looks down with pity on us who know no better than to like pipe organs and violins; who — count two — worships a strange god, although his father is ·reported to have been a Christian missionary; who —count three — speaks English fluently and a dozen other unfamiliar languages equally well. Let's see — you are charged with knowing four or five dialects of Arabic, Berber, Armenian, Tatar, Persian, and Turkish, that's a rather mysterious assortment of tongues; and who — count four — is greeted by a Russian revolutionist as comrade and also speaks that language, which I forgot to mention; and — count five — owns Aladdin's lamp, claps his hands, and produces a full-blown Oriental banquet in a New York studio. Now if all this does not constitute a Man of Mystery, I don't know what the phrase means."·

Lane was a bit dazed by this long bill of indictment, but, as Eunice had said to Helen, he was not at all afraid of men. Besides he had decided that he wanted to be friends with these people. On the whole he was amused at the speculation he had unwittingly aroused.

"I am afraid I must plead guilty to an unusual facility for languages," he said apologetically. "But it really is not my fault. I seem to have been born with it. All the rest is commonplace enough. I am .

sorry I did not make it clear at first. I read in a book on etiquette that it was not good form to talk about oneself. But if you are interested, I will tell you my history."

"Go to it," Pete said.

"And don't make it too brief," Lancaster put in.

"The night is young yet," Win added.

"Oh, do not worry. There is nothing in my story to keep you up late. My life has been very interesting to me, but I do not think it will be to others. I do not know exactly when I was born — a little more than thirty years ago — in Marakesh —'Morocco City,' your English maps call it. My parents had gone there as missionaries. My mother died when I was a baby. I do not remember her. My father, who was a doctor, died when I was about fifteen. He never told me about my childhood, so I am vague about that. Perhaps I had been baptized a Christian. I do not know. But long before I can remember, my father had become a Mohammedan. In my earliest recollections, we were Muslims. I went ——"

"If you don't mind being cross-questioned," McGee interrupted, "I'd like to ask about your father. It isn't often that a missionary embraces the religion he started out to combat. Why did he change?"

Lane considered a moment.

"I am not altogether sure myself. You see I was only a boy when my father died. It seemed so natural to me to be a Mohammedan — I did not know any Christians — that I never asked him about it. And yet I think I understand.

"As I remember him, the reality of his religion

was a passion to help people in pain. He was like Abou Ben Adhem, in your poem, he loved his fellow men. I do not know why he first went out as a missionary. Perhaps he had heard that there was a great need for doctors in Morocco. Perhaps my mother, whom he loved very much, was more devout.

"When she died, my father did not want to leave her alone in a strange land. He often said he wanted to be buried beside her. And when he had decided to live there all the rest of his life, I think he felt that he could serve his fellow men better, that he could have a greater influence for good, could more easily cure the ills of their bodies, if he were really one of them. And so he became a Muslim. At least this is how I think he felt.

"It would not seem so strange to you, if you knew Mohammedan countries. In the Levant there are many native Christians — Armenians, Syrians, Greeks, Copts, and Bulgars. When the missionaries there find that they cannot make converts of the Mohammedans, they turn to these native Christians and do much good for them in their hospitals and schools. Most of the missionaries I have known are good people. I imagine that they find it easier to be Christians among us than here in America. In the East, we respect all people who sincerely try to find God, even if we think they are on the wrong path.

"But in Morocco there are no native Christians. The missionaries in Marakesh have a few orphan boys and girls in their school, but when I was there last they had only one adult convert — and I do not think they are very proud of him. They have a doctor

there now; he tries very hard to do good. But the
people will not go to him because, in such very bad
-Arabic, he tells them things about their religion
which are not true. Even here in a Christian land,
I do not think that you would go to a doctor who was
more interested in your soul than in your stomach or
your sore finger or whatever it was that was hurting
you."

"You needn't deal tenderly with the missionaries,"
Win said. "We don't subscribe to foreign missions.
We're trying to put our own house in order."

"There is another thing in Morocco which perhaps
influenced my father. Outside of the half dozen missionaries, there are very few decent Christians. I
think that if you had to live there — after you had
got to know the Europeans — you would not like to
be called a Christian. They are dishonest merchants,
their word cannot be trusted, and they make vice an
open show in our streets. And also they are drunk-
ards. My father was a great believer in temperance.
And our people never touch alcohol — except in the
coast towns like Tangier, where contact with Christians has debauched them. My father often spoke to
me of that.

"I do not know just what was in my father's mind
when he went into the mosque to pray. I think religion is more a matter of feeling than of reason. If
a person has thought about theology till he has lost
faith in the God of his childhood, I doubt if he will
ever believe very deeply in another god. I do not
know whether my father was a really devout Muslim.
Perhaps he had been a sort of Christian Agnostic and

became a Mohammedan Agnostic. He was too much of a scientist to give much weight to dogmas. It did not matter to him what people he served nor what they believed. He was glad to help them with what skill and instruments and drugs he had.

"As I said, I do not know whether he was exactly orthodox in his theology. But as far back as I can remember he was a *Maraboo*, a saint. He did good to every one and every one loved him. Even now — even in far-away corners of the mountains — I am sure to be treated kindly because I am my father's son.

"There is a legend among the people that he was buried beside his wife. He was not. But many people come to her grave to pray. It is, perhaps, funny, Mohammedans praying beside the tomb of a Christian woman. But it makes me very proud of my father.

"He always spoke English to me and taught me to read and write. He intended to send me to America to study medicine. And I went to the school of his Zawïa ——"

"What's a Zawïa?"

"Oh, there are many sects in Islam — somewhat like your religious orders. My father belonged to the Khaderïa. They are followers of Muley Abd el-Khader el-Jilani, a saint who lived in the twelfth century of your era. He is the patron of beggars and all who are in need. He was a good deal like St. Francis d'Assisi. Each chapter house — Zawïa — has a school for the children of the members. They are not very good schools, only the language and the Koran.

"So I learned the classic Arabic at school and the

Marakesh dialect from the boys, and my foster-mother
was a Berber woman from the Ṣous Valley. The book
I am now working on is a collection of the songs and
stories she taught me. The Berber folklore is very
interesting. Long ago they worshiped a female
deity — the Astarte of the Phœnicians. They are a
Semitic people. Many of their epics and stories have
a heroine instead of a hero. Of course that was long
before they became Christians."

"Didn't you say that there weren't any native
Christians?" Win asked.

"Oh, there are none now. The Berbers were
Christians under the Roman Empire — for several
hundred years before Mohammed was born. But by
the end of the seventh century of your era they were
converted to Islam.

"When I was about fifteen my father took me on
the Hadj to Mecca. Almost all the Christian books
on Islam speak lightly of the Pilgrimage. It seems
strange to me that you, who make so much of conven-
tions — hardly a day passes when some of you do not
rush off to a congress or conference, sometimes halfway around the world — it is strange that you do not
understand how important the Pilgrimage is to us.
It is the General Assembly of our Church, a Parlia-
ment of Nations for political discussions, a conference
of savants, a tournament of poetry, all rolled into
one. It is the strongest unifying force of our civili-
zation. I think it was the wisest and most states-
manlike thing our Prophet did for us.

"It was at Mecca that I first became really interested in languages. I met boys whose speech I could

not understand. I learned a good deal of Afghan from one of them and from another some of a language I have never been able to identify. Perhaps it was some obscure, unstudied Malay dialect.

"The plague was bad that year — worse than usual. On the way home there was an epidemic in one of the Syrian ports. I do not remember which one, nor how we got there. Of course we stopped. Father, being a doctor, had to. There were some missionary doctors also who came to fight the plague. They were the first people, besides my father and a man on the street in Cairo, with whom I had ever talked English. I suppose father told them who he was. Anyhow, when he caught the plague, he asked them to take care of me and give me an education. He always wanted me to be a doctor.

"He died there. It was very sad; he could not be buried beside my mother.

"I do not remember very well what happened after that. I did not care. There was almost a fight between our Moorish friends and the missionaries over who should take care of me. I did not want to go with the strangers. But my father had wished it, so I did. They took me to their school at Beirut. They were very good to me. I remember especially one woman — so kind! — like a mother, I suppose. I do not remember my own. But they tried to make a Christian of me. I was only a youngster, about fifteen. I thought my father was the best and wisest man who had ever lived. He was a Mohammedan. All the people I had ever known thought it was horrible for a Muslim to become a renegade. So, as they would not let me alone, I ran away. When I got to Constantinople——"

"Hold on," McGee interrupted. "How did you get to Constantinople? I don't suppose you stole the foreign mission funds to buy a steamer ticket, and you haven't told us yet about finding the Magic Carpet."

"Oh, now," Lane protested, laughing. "You must not look for mysteries. It is the easiest thing in the world to be a tramp in the East. Especially return- ing from the Hadj. We have no laws against vagrants. It is permitted to beg. You can sleep in the mosques and nearly everywhere I would find a Zawïa of the Khaderïa. And sometimes I worked. I went overland across Asia Minor. I suppose it took me about six months to get to Constantinople."

"And there I fell into luck — a job, as guide, for a family of American tourists. It was funny. Con- stantinople is a big city — the largest I had ever seen. I did not know my way about, but on the road I had picked up a good deal of Turkish — enough to ask questions. Every morning I would go up to their hotel. Perhaps they would say that they wanted to visit the mosque of Akmet. I had never heard of it. 'Yes,' I would say, 'Alonce, veree queek.' I was afraid to speak good English in those days for fear they would try to make a Christian of me. I would put them in a cab and get up beside the driver and on the way I would ask him to tell me about the Mosque of Akmet. They never suspected how little I knew about Constantinople.

"One day they wanted to go out to Robert College on the Bosporus. I had heard about it at Beirut.

Milton Keynes UK
Ingram Content Group UK Ltd.
UKHW022241131223
434291UK00007B/582